Running On Ice
FROM TRAGEDY TO TRIUMPH

Running On Ice
From Tragedy to Triumph

Joanne P. Humbles

XULON PRESS

Xulon Press
2301 Lucien Way #415
Maitland, FL 32751
407.339.4217
www.xulonpress.com

© 2020 by Joanne P. Humbles

All rights reserved solely by the author. The author guarantees all contents are original and do not infringe upon the legal rights of any other person or work. No part of this book may be reproduced in any form without the permission of the author. The views expressed in this book are not necessarily those of the publisher.

Unless otherwise indicated, Scripture quotations taken from the King James Version (KJV) – *public domain*.

Scripture quotations taken from the The Holy Bible, Berean Literal Bible (BLB). Copyright ©2016, 2018 by Bible Hub. sed by Permission. All Rights Reserved Worldwide.

Scripture quotations taken from the Holy Bible, New International Version (NIV). Copyright © 1973, 1978, 1984, 2011 by Biblica, Inc.™. Used by permission. All rights reserved.

Printed in the United States of America

Paperback ISBN-13: 978-1-6628-0137-2
Hard Cover ISBN-13: 978-1-6628-0138-9
Ebook ISBN-13: 978-1-6628-0139-6

Preview:

When I stepped off the elevator on the third floor the doors opened at the Nurses' Station. There was a doctor standing behind the desk speaking with the nurses. I thought it odd that he would have his surgical gear, mask, lab coat and gloves on behind the desk at the nurses' station. I saw small splats of blood on his clothes. Then I noticed that they were whispering, and I heard the nurse tell him, "There is Mrs. Humbles now!" The surgeon calmly pulled down his mask and walked towards me, to introduce himself. I cannot adequately describe the horrible feeling I got in the pit of my stomach at that moment to this very day. He escorted me to a side conference room, and he asked me to please sit down. I sat down and he sat across from me in a chair facing me. He began with, "I'm sorry to inform you that Terrance is going to die."

Also Authored by Joanne P Horne: **God's Laws and Business,** *"Wisdom is the principal thing; therefore, get wisdom: and with all your getting get understanding." Proverb 4:11*

Copyright 4/26/12
ISBN 978-1-4497-4893-7

The strongest oak of the forest is not the one that is protected from the storm and hidden from the sun. It's the one that stands in the open where it is compelled to struggle for its existence against the winds and rains and the scorching sun.

Napoleon Hill

DEDICATION

This book is dedicated to my deceased ex-husband and dear brother in Christ Terrance Humbles, my son Sean, and my lovely daughter Faith. All of you have been wonderful and equally supportive to each other through this difficult but necessary period in our lives.

Contents

PREFACE . . . . *xiii*
1. When November Ends. 1
2. And In The Meantime...Conspiracy! 8
3. The New Year Recovering 17
4. On The Bay. 23
5. I Had To Bear It 30
6. Squeeze The Big Red Pillow,
   When You Cough 34
7. A Friend In Your Need Is A Friend Indeed. 45
8. Trouble Brewing 49
9. His Grace Is Sufficient 63
10. It's A Long Way Home. 78
11. He Was Caught Up to Meet Him. 83
12. Killing Me Softly 97
13. Three Strikes You're Out! 100
14. Intense Battles 110
15. Our Gain. 115
16. The Things We Kept. 119
In Conclusion. 133
References 137

Preface
HIGH PLATEAUS AND FLAT PLAINS

Through the years, there were nights when would go to bed and turn our faces away from each other to cry. One of us not wanting the other to know that they were crying. Crying about the illness, the constant pressure to make critical health decisions. There was always another operation, always another emergency, another stroke, another doctor, another reason to worry, a legitimate reason to be afraid. The transition from being strong, vibrant and healthy to becoming permanently disable was an emotionally painful one. Oh, how we cried... to witness health flee at the age of forty-three. We couldn't subdue it, just couldn't hold on to it. It left.

Through the battles we carried our past scars, wore them like badges. We were losing but we kept on fighting. There was more infection, another heart attack, another artery blockage or collapse, another day of mourning of new bad news. We tried to believe that God knew just what was going on in our lives and that he would see us through. We embraced the probability that this was his will. We prayed always. We sincerely believed that God would deliver us from our issues.

I wasn't sure if I wanted time to stand still or to skip forward. Standing still meant wrestling with the anticipation of upcoming trials and the expectation of the things that could come, which was agony. Skipping forward meant plunging into deep waters. There never seemed to be just a puddle to piddle through. There was always a deep murky muddy river to cross. Who would have predicted that wading through these swamps in life would educate and prepare us to become tour guides? Guides for other explorers. This was a life learning experience. One sure to bring forth expertise. We discovered what could be lurking in waters. Be a river or a swamp, we would discover what could lie beneath. Every poisonous reptile, every vile, slimy, creeping thing beneath the murky waters sank its fangs into us but God was faithful not to allow the water to overflow us. As he promised by prophet Isaiah found in

Isaiah 43:2 KJV

"When thou passest through the waters, I will be with thee; and through the rivers, they shall not overflow thee: when thou walkest through the fire, thou shalt not be burned; neither shall the flame kindle upon thee.

But there were other times when we could relate to Paul after he survived a shipwreck and swam to the island of Melita. He had gathered a bundle of sticks, and laid them on the fire, there came a viper out of the heat, and fastened on his hand, they said among themselves, no doubt this man is a murderer, whom, though he hath escaped the sea, yet vengeance suffer him not to live. Then he shook off the beast in the fire and felt no harm. Every time we got comfortable with a routine with the next level of illness, medication adjusted, able to walk again, able to talk again and resting comfortably it proved to be a futile posterity.

There was always one more mountain to climb. Every new mountain possessed increasingly uncertain resting places on the cliffs. Sharper edges to grab onto during the more challenging points of the climb. Caves high in the rock provided a secure place to sleep, overlooking rushing streams of waters which flowed through the rocks. These caves provided physical resting places but little rest or water for the soul. Every mountain had its own disastrous weather conditions. On some mountains we experienced thunderstorms that packed strong winds and rains, some blizzards, and some avalanches. One thing consistent on all the mountains was, with the increase of altitude, an increase of oxygen was necessary for survival. These mountains that seemed impossible to climb became a part of a living portrait, painted by a gifted artist. Destined to become the conversation piece in the middle of our dinner table. The great creator, GOD ALMIGHTY, laid out a clean canvas, chose his colors, and drafted a landscape. He painted images on the canvas of destiny and mounted it on the wall in the living room of our lives.

Expecting the unexpected became a part of our daily routine. Enjoying life for the way it was, everyday that it was. What was living anyway but experiencing ourselves? We had to accept what was, and pass on the things that were not, at least for the moment anyway. Hoping that things were the way they use to be became a fleeing thought. Nothing to hold onto. Life was forever changing. The ground we had covered could not be re-explored (too dangerous) ... Some of the open pits were now camouflaged by grass, we were sure to fall into them this time. We were not the same weight that we were when we stepped over them the first time.

We had collected things from the paths that we thought might be useful to us along the way. Things that other explorers discarded became our prized possessions. An old shoe here, a pair of broken specks, a box of matches there, items that other people disposed of after their practical use. Where they were headed next, they were sure they were useless. They need not carry shoes, glasses or the such. At a point, we realized that we were carrying more baggage, more than we started with. We felt the weight, and it was so much more than we started off with. Some finds were useful, others were tossed further down the road. We carried them just in case we needed them. Life has a way of teaching you to collect and compelling you to discard. We collect in preparation for the journey a head, we discard in preparation for the end of our journeys. Where we are on the trail of life, raw instinct instructs us to prepare.

Chapter 1
WHEN NOVEMBER ENDS

Isn't it funny that we are able to remember details of good experiences, as well as, the unfortunate events that we encounter in the course of living our lives? How ingeniously crafted is the human body, especially the mind. Designed with the ability to recall and relive what we experience with the same physical sensations that we felt during those exact occurrences. Equipped with an internal invisible emotional weight scale, carefully distributing the weight with such accuracy, hitting a perfect balance. Not giving us the ability to experience one memory more than the other against our own wills. It is obvious, that our creator possessed far more intelligence and genius than the creation. If left up to man to choose, I am sure we would choose to remember the good and to forget the bad. I must agree with Ralph Waldo Emerson when he quoted, *"Bad times have a scientific value. These are occasions, a good learner would not miss".* Our greatest lessons are packaged within and extracted from our bad times. They teach us to identify, appreciate and enjoy our good times.

It was a brisk sunny November morning. November 4th, 2000, which appeared to be a great day. A day of celebration, my son's 18th birthday. His formal introduction to manhood, a day that the family had planned on making a memorable one. And wow, did it turn out to be just that. My husband rose early rushing to work so that he could complete his route early and prepare for the festivities. He wanted to make his own contribution to the day, *"for the boy was coming into his own,"* as some people would say… Little did we know that life would require it of him from that day to this one. The Events that followed called his maturity to the forefront. I awoke with a busy mind, pick-up the cake, pick-up some gifts, pick-up the ingredients for his favorite foods for dinner. I was on call for the job, my daughter had to have her hair done and grandma had some errands to run while I was out. Oh yeah, the house had to be cleaned. It was Saturday morning, the busiest day of the week. At about 1:00pm I received a call from Terry, my husband. As soon as I heard his voice on the phone, I thought of a list of things I needed him to do on his way home. Before I could say anything, he informed me that he was at Central Suffolk Hospital. He had left work early to check out this pain he had in his chest, but not to worry, as soon as they release him, he was returning to work so that he could get home to us. That's when I heard a different voice on the phone, it was the emergency room nurse. She asked me to come to the hospital to be with my husband because he presented with chest pain, sweating, pain radiating up the left arm and nausea. He had been given a TPA shot to break clots and cause blood to begin to flow smoothly through the heart again. The pain had begun to subside. He had suffered a heart attack and he would not be released for a few days. A heart attack. This man was 43yrs old. A Certified Personal Trainer, who's career path consisted of positions such as the Recreation Director and the Sports Coordinator for a number of agencies over the past thirty years. He worked out everyday. He was currently lifting 335lbs at the gym... Physical exercise was the joy of his life. He got out of daily exercise what most people don't, enjoyment. I was devastated. Partly because I realized that something had transpired that would change our lives, but mostly because I could feel his devastation. I knew that Terry took great pleasure in building his body and showing off what he was able to attain, without much effort at all. He was a natural. All of that was behind him now. No more weights or workouts at the gym. For him, I sensed that this was something so unacceptable, this simply had not happened, in his mind. When I arrived, he surprised me with his *(it's nothing to worry about, I'm alright)* humor, but that was certainly not the case. The hospital transferred him up to the Intensive Care Unit for close observation. After 3 days he was transferred to a hospital that specialized in heart procedures. The doctor was suspecting more blockages. He was right. Terry had a clot in an artery in the front of the heart and another clot in an artery in the rear of the heart. He also had sustained substantial damage to the bottom of his heart muscle. He was hooked up to an intravenous drip of Heparin among other medications in hope of dissolving the clots before stents could be placed in the arteries. Upon hearing this we prayed and pleaded with God. For approximately

4 days he was on the Heparin drip, on the 5th day the doctor took him in to surgery in hopes of possibly breaking up the clots by force and placing the stents in the arteries. He received 4 stents. During the hours of his surgery I fasted. I was determined to touch the heart of God. My sister Yvonne arrived at the hospital and was amazed with the fact that I was there alone and unafraid to hear what the surgeon would say upon completion. When you have to be strong through a personal storm, you will be impressed with how much stress you can actually stand up under. You handle it when you have to. There is a statement that people make to others when they want to encourage them to give it the best they've got and it goes like this, *"Show me what you're made of."* Well, there will be periods in your life where you will have to 'give it all you've got', especially if you are the only one involved that has anything to give. The best in people are magnified at these times and so is the worst. **During times of great duress and tension, you should discipline yourself to be on your best behavior because the inner qualities that you display will be forever remembered, by the people you have to deal with, the Good and certainly the Bad. Most people do**

not believe that they have to be courteous to the Doctors or the rest of the hospital staff for that matter. We believe that because we pay the salary of the professionals involved, they can mistreat them. Keep in mind that it's a good thing to have the support and respect of the doctor and that you support and respect him while he is caring for you or your loved one. I personally would not want anyone to perform surgery on or care for me that do not think I am worthy of their care. Do yourself a favor and dish out what you expect to get back. Between God and the staff, your life is literately in their hands. Good moral character is something that most people want to mirror when they are being presented it. You can set the tone.

Regurgitating the words of Horace, **"When things are steep, remember to stay level-headed".**

The hospital was 1 hour and 15 minutes away from our home, *so I stayed there*, not to mention Terry's fear of hospitals. After the first night in the patient lounge sleeping in an inflexible upright plastic chair and some good ole' sympathy from the 2nd floor nursing station, I got a Lazy Boy chair with wheels and a few blankets at about 8:00pm every night. Each morning I would freshen up in the ladies' room before scurrying down the hall to sit with Terry. He was terribly afraid of what could happen considering what was happening. He had gone through two angiograms and an angioplasty. The next day Terry was released. We were ecstatic to be on our way home. We were going home. But what appeared to be an ending to a horrible experience was really the beginning of a series of more risky and complicated surgeries.

Chapter 2

And In The Meantime...
Conspiracy!

During the time that all these events were occurring there were other things going on behind the scene. I was working for a well known company as a Senior Data Marketing Support Specialist. Upon coming on with the company, my background was extensive, and my qualifications were above reproach. After working for the company a few years, I began to address what I viewed as inappropriate and degrading racially motivated practices from the staff, as well as, the management. I complained to my superiors and discovered that they had no intention to fully follow company policy nor were they open to conform to Federal Racial Discrimination Laws. I was patient with my bosses, initially attributing their behavior to their own inexperience in management. But this I found, was not the case as the story played itself out. Shortly before my husband's episode, he watched me become increasingly disgusted and disappointed with my inability to reach these people. At a point he even helped me develop a list of issues to be addressed in my meetings. The list was designed to help me remember and to help me not to negate to discuss the important issues in the heat of the moment. Well, the pressure got so high at home, we began to talk over these issues often to relieve tension. I had absolutely no intention of leaving my job or losing it. Three days before my husband suffered the heart attack, I found myself standing in the hallway at the company complaining about how embarrassed I was after having been handed a joke that was sexually explicate and racially degrading. I had been complaining previously about this type of behavior. The employee who gave me a copy also handed a copy to two of our managers and a few other white male employees. This was proof positive in my opinion, that this employee was obviously out of control but felt quite comfortable with his own actions. After I had a meeting on Nov 3rd with the manager of my department, we suffered the ultimate sacrifice, Terry's health. But, first things first, I took care of my husband first. The employee who gave me the joke even had the nerve to show up at the hospital. He claimed he had a friend in the hospital. What an awful surprise, not to mention he came during the period that Terry was receiving a Heparin drip to dissolve blood clots in his heart. Not a good time to visit, you think? I spotted him in the hallway first and advised my husband to stay calm... He had already said to me that he would feel more comfortable if he picked me up from work everyday because of the hostility that came as a result of my complaints. And now here at the hospital, is one of the main characters involved in the ruckus. And here he is, walking into Terry's room. How dare he come to see if what I had reported was true, Terry was furious. But he was also in danger of having a massive heart attack. He had to stay calm, which before now was not an option, not one that he would consider anyway. Terry wanted to confront him about it. He wanted to make him apologize to me, his wife...

Stress is a killer. We have heard the US Department of Health Department tell us, our doctors tell us, and the statistics combined of millions of people who have become diseased and disabled every year by it tells us. We really do not understand until we personally suffer because of it. According to WebMD.com web site,

- Forty-three percent of all adults suffer adverse health effects from stress.
- Seventy-five percent to 90% of all doctor's office visits are for stress-related ailments and complaints.
- Stress can play a part in problems such as headaches, high blood pressure, heart problems, diabetes, skin conditions, asthma, arthritis, depression, and anxiety.
- The Occupational Safety and Health Administration (OSHA) declared stress a hazard of the workplace. Stress costs American industry more than $300 billion annually.
- The lifetime prevalence of an emotional disorder is more than 50%, often due to chronic, untreated stress reactions.

Some stressors are unavoidable, and some stress is directed at us deliberately, wearing us down. Whether it is unavoidable or deliberate, stress must be handled properly. Most stressors are not worth the pressure that we allow to build up within us. We worry and stress over things that if we allow them to, will naturally work out.

This also turned into the beginning of a long and lengthy relationship between us and the Workman's Compensation board. Workman's Compensation was to pay him weekly as Terry would be temporarily out of work, so we all thought. It sounded easy, too easy...

After the hospital stay with Terry, I returned to work to find, to my dismay, the employee that handed me the joke and visited my husband in the hospital still sharing a cubical with me. The company's policy had been violated and I felt that the issue had not been addressed seeing that no reprimand had been given to the violator. I was becoming angry, very angry. But primarily, I thought that if this employee was allowed to get away with this action, there would be more of this behavior to follow. That day I ran into some female colleagues from my department in the ladies' room having a huddle. Evidently, they had heard of the incident and they wanted to bet me that there would be no consequences for the offender. He had a long history of violating company policy and getting away with it. I e-mailed the personnel director to see if my manager had notified her regarding the incident before leaving on November 3rd for the weekend, if so, I was interested in hearing what steps had been taken to assure me that this behavior would not be tolerated as per company policy. I wanted the buck to stop there… This joke was, what I thought, to be the fuel that the company needed to believe that my previous complaints were legitimate and true. That was not to be. I was called into the Vice President's office. When I enter the office, he asked me to sit down. The Vice President conferenced in the personnel director from Chicago. She preceded to tell me that she had in fact interviewed my colleagues and they had no complaints, and that my complaints were unwarranted, and I was probably over sensitive because of my husband's illness, she said that she had not been offended by the joke. She was also a black American female, an uncompensated obstruction. I felt as if she had been assigned to me for the sole purpose of convincing me that what I was experiencing was a ridiculous erroneous belief. This was something that no one else was experiencing, but me. Personnel suggested that I contact the employee assistance program for mental and emotional help. I was appalled… I realized at that point that I was alone, there was no internal support for me, or protection for that matter. From that moment, I understood that I would have to be watchful and responsible for my safety at work. Other black and Indian employees began to distance themselves from me as if they were thinking the same thought as myself. These people understood that if the company was not behind me, they themselves cannot be if they planned to keep their jobs. They understood that blacklisting was my destiny with the company, and possibly with my career of engineering, all together. I was in trouble. But this was far from over… There was a trap laid for me. We, African Americans who thought this was behind us in this country, not so. I realized that the players involved were discussing handling me and not the violation. I was their problem and that's when I began to fear. I was the defense and the offense was about fifty people strong. I knew I would become an out cast and ostracized or I would be pressured to leave, which would have been playing into their hands. The latter was the preference for them. I chose the former. How could they do this to me? Surely, they saw that I would keep quite and that I desperately needed them to understand my situation. Surely, they knew my husband was out of work receiving disability and that I was the sole support of my family. I began to really watch myself at this point. I felt as if I had to be at work at exactly the minute, I was schedule to work. And I had to work hard when I was there and prove to them that I could continue to do my job well and shut my mouth about what I saw. I had my own problems and wanted no trouble. I was determined to keep my job... My daughter was in Catholic School and my son was in College. Not to mention that Terry's medicine was paid- in cash because Workmen's Compensation wasn't covering it. We were constantly in court with Workmen's Compensation trying to force them to honor their orders from the State Board to pay his medical bills and give him an income until he returned to work. They argued that he would be at work and that it is the responsibility of the hospital for any further damage outside of the initial heart attack. The hospital had caused some damage to the heart, but the initial heart attack was at work. So, we went around and around in the ring. They were finally ordered to pay for all of his medical care and also pay him a monthly income payment for the rest of his life. Which meant they were responsible for his medical and financial care for the rest of his life. The Workmen Compensation doctors had determined that due to the severity of Terry's medical condition, the extensive number of doses a day and the strengths of those medications would cut his life span to 57years old, no greater than 61 years old.

Chapter 3
THE NEW YEAR RECOVERING

CHRISTMAS CAME QUICKLY AND TERRY 's, rehabilitation was finish. He was still not feeling up to snuff. He was walking around the house, but not fast. The doctors told him to exercise and in three weeks he should get back to everyday activities. Terry joked about his condition; he was anxious to resume his life. His diet was changed, and his body was feeling somewhat better. He was confident in his ability to command his body to recover. To his dismay his body was doing what it wanted to do. It seemed foreign to Terry that he was not feeling well. He was hearing a clicking noise in his chest, which we were sure would disappear. We began to shop for Christmas, and I noticed Terry not being able to quite keep up with me. There was not a chance that I would allow him to lift anything that was heavy. Terry also noticed that when he got angry or stressed, he felt pressure in his chest. We began to think that the stents were not living up to their reputation of at least five years of success. They simply were not feeling normal. On Christmas morning we were awakened by my daughter. She was always the first one up on Christmas. She automatically assumed she had the best presents and certainly they were the most fun. Her brother and our only son was eleven years her elder. His age was getting him presents, given to young men. While watching the children opening their presents, I just happen to notice Terry looking very tired and his face bore a gray overtone on it. I watched him during the day as he was careful moving around. About noon that day Terry told me that he was having light pressure and pain in his chest, I became nervous immediately. I imaged seeing him fall on the Christmas tree and dying before the children on Christmas day. I wanted to take him to the emergency room immediately. Terry assured me that he could wait until the next morning. We waited and the rest of that day felt like a year. I called the doctor and he wanted us to come to the emergency, he would meet us there for testing. While we traveled back to the hospital we prayed. When we arrived at the hospital and the doctor gave Terry an angiogram and

The New Year Recovering

found that there was another artery that needed a stent. They then placed a fifth stent inside of his heart. He felt much better right after the operation. We went home the next morning.

We met the dawning of a New Year recovering from the insertion of another stent. But on January 3rd Terry was back in the local hospital's emergency room for chest pain. His General Practitioner met us there. On the electro-cardiogram he saw an introverted sign wave. Terry spent the night on a stretcher in the emergency room and then he was transferred back to the hospital that specialized in heart surgery. He was transported by ambulance with a referral for another angiogram. The following morning, he was given an angiogram and it was determined that the stents had not shifted causing him discomfort. We were sent home disappointed because nothing was found and because Terry was still not feeling well. The doctors began to believe that the medications may be toxic in his system, so they began to test him in order to adjust them. They found nothing... Our Surgical Cardiologist referred us to a local Cardiologist for our follow-ups. Once we changed the Cardiologist Terry began having problems with his heart rate.

This new doctor strapped a heart monitor on him. A few days later the report came back to normal. We made a six-week appointment. The doctor set Terry up for an echo cardiogram and a stress test. Terry took these tests and the test looked suspect, so we found ourselves back at the hospital to get another angiogram. The doctor administering the angiogram found nothing unusual, everything looked fine. We were sent back to the cardiologist, but Terry felt that there was still something desperately wrong. He was having chest discomfort, jaw discomfort, and he was constantly exhausted. The doctor wanted Terry to return back to work but Terry asked the doctor if he could have cardiac rehabilitation. Workman's compensation decided to stop his payments. Oh, the pressure and financial burden that caused us. They were trying to force Terry to do something he could not do. Terry hired a lawyer in an attempt to stop the madness. Workman's Compensation still stopped the payments. The secretary at Terry's place of employment said that he would not be eligible because the injury was a heart injury, we disagreed. I had only one regret from all of this and that was telling my colleagues from my job.

I notified my supervisors assuming that they would be sympathetic to my situation. I really don't know what I thought they might do. Even I began to question if Terry was really feeling that ill. Terry was trying to buy time, to prove that there was a problem, still. The doctor sent Terry to a Rehabilitation Center in Southampton Town. At the Rehabilitation Center the director watched Terry's heart rate and blood pressure while exercising and determined that he was not going to be allowed to continue until he receives an angiogram because she felt something was wrong with his heart. SOOO, we headed back to the doctor who referred us back to the surgeon. He had another angiogram this time the surgeon found some stenosis in two of the arteries that already had stents. At this time one artery had only 25% blockage and another had 30% blockage. The surgeon decided to do nothing but prescribe nitroglycerine and wait, by this time it was April 2001. Terry took nitroglycerine when he felt pain. Sometimes two or three times a day. He had been prescribed nitroglycerine since the January incident, but he rarely took it. In May Terry had another episode and another angiogram, which confirmed the doctor's fears. His arteries were 75% full of stenosis in one and 95 in another, then a third was about 30%. The surgeon informed us that we needed desperately to take the by-pass surgery. The only other option was death. The surgeon set us up for consultation with the chief cardiologist who would perform the surgery.

Chapter 4
ON THE BAY

Considering the surgeon diagnosis, bypass surgery was necessary. We decided to take a day off together and go to the beach. Terry was terribly troubled about the operation; he did not want anyone to break open his rib cage. He had worked out all his adult life, and now after such dedication and determination to make his body perfect, this. He had made the decision earlier not to have open heart surgery. Terry had this strange feeling that he was not going to be all right. We drove down to the Jamesport Bay and we discussed what he wanted me to do if anything went wrong in surgery. We discussed how far he wanted me to go if he were to need a respirator? Did he want me to try to keep him alive or let him go on to glory? If he ended up in a vegetative state, would he desire life support and to live a life of restriction? Could he live without his natural body function? Better yet, would he want to live without his body? We talked about the children and how this was bound to affect them. We had a son beginning college and a seven-year-old daughter, and they both needed both of us. But most of all, we were inseparable, we never went any place other than work without each other. If you see one of us, you would see us both. This was something that had never occurred to us, nothing that we made an effort to do. We just did it. When one of us ran to the store the other went to keep each other company. What now? Things were changing we could sense it in the atmosphere. We were the couple who finished each others' sentences. Little did we know that change would come so suddenly. I think, if we foresaw this coming, we would have tried to avoid part of the adjustment that came later on, by simply insisting that we do things without each person. I took so many small things for granted like going out at night and then coming back in. I always had Terry who was so patient, with me. If I had to go out six times in a night, he would go with me for protection. I did the same with him. We did everything together. We went to every event together, all the children's school events. We went to every bar-b-que, every church service, all of our vacations, every carnival, grocery stores, everywhere. One did not want to go if the other was not going. These are the things that immediately changed after the operation. Sometimes we have relationships that are rare to find, and we take it for granted believing that everyone has the same relationships. We discover that we had much more after what we have is gone. ***It's wise to take inventory occasionally just to get a clear perspective of your circumstances.*** You are then able to appreciate your state of affairs. Life is short demanding that the teacher has to teach quickly. Today we have youth, tomorrow we have old age, if we are fortunate enough to attain it.

Terry instructed me that whatever I do, do not disconnect the respirator. He wanted to live at all cost. There were no other choices to be considered. I was a bit surprised at his answer, knowing he was very conceited, even vain about his body. He would strut as if he was the only rooster in the hen house, and people took notice. His muscles in his arms and legs were huge and perfectly sculptured, he was proud. He loved the way he looked and prided himself in his knowledge of physical education and exercise. I was never into that much physical exercise. Just enough to keep the weight down. Isn't that always the way it is? Everybody else is attracted to what your partner possess but his or her mate can either take it or leave it. But Terry was soon to understand why the apostle Paul wrote to the church in

1 Tim: 4:8 KJV

For bodily exercise profiteth little: but godliness is profitable unto all things, having promise of the life that now is, and of that which is to come.

Exercise was good but it had very little to offer if you really got sick and could not continue in it. It had absolutely no effect on your spiritual growth. It is not beneficial in all things. There were occasions that it could offer nothing at all. As does everything else, exercise has its place. Unfortunately, it's place for him, would surprisingly be through physical therapy.

As we watched the waves rolling gently onto the shore and sneaking back out to bay, we tried to pre-plan, draw a schematic to follow in the next few weeks. We searched nature for some direction. We examine the sky for solace, we searched the rich scenery of the forest for consent to go on, we listened intently to the sounds of bay for a sure path. We searched within ourselves for a still small voice of instruction, bona fide answers. We found nothing. It seemed as if our ability to receive was dead. Where was God...? Was he remotely aware that we needed his advice? If He was not paying attention to us now, He might miss the whole ordeal. The idea of being hung out to dry was very troubling to us, we needed Him, and we needed Him now. There was nothing we could do to comfort ourselves or each other, for that matter. We needed assurance that the steps we were about to take were sure ones. Falling in any direction was risky. We felt as if we were climbing up this rocky mountain and looking up the path before us appeared so dark and unsure. The next stone we grabbed hold of for leverage could be the stone that would hurl us to our death. All the ledges we used to hoist ourselves up by, had given way, we had to go forward, for there was no room on the path to turn around. The only foothold we were sure of was the one we had our foot in but the stones which held it together was crumbling and would soon give way. Our weight was more than it could bear. We had to move on to the uncertain areas that were above us. The altitude was becoming greater and the air was thinning. We felt the panic that accompanies asphyxiation, the killer being our own physical limitations. We were victims trapped inside of ourselves. We had no control over the air density up there. **Air density**, like **air** pressure, decreases with increasing altitude. It also changes with variation in atmospheric pressure, temperature and humidity.

Healthy bodies can adapt to the challenges of high altitude remarkably well. Breathing becomes faster and deeper to take in more oxygen, the heart beats faster and pumps harder to propel more oxygen to the tissues, and the sympathetic nervous system pours out more adrenaline to meet the stress. During weeks and months of high-altitude living, the bone marrow produces more oxygen-carrying red blood cells, and the circulatory overactivity settles down. But until acclimatization occurs, the stresses of altitude can tax the heart and lungs, particularly if they're not entirely healthy to begin with. As it was with us.

We were officially into cyclic altitude ascension.

Chapter 5
I Had To Bear It

During this period of time I was also treading lightly at my job. Being careful to cross all my t's and dot my i's. I was right when I thought I was working under a microscope. At this point I began to feel that my desk phone was being monitored and my e-mail watched. This turned out to be true according to the evidence obtained from the company in the discovery period as a result of litigation in a racial bias case I filed against them. I really began to feel the pressure of having to take my husband to his doctors' appointments. The supervisors was watching my time off like hawks. They began to monitor my personal phone calls. I felt that they were trying to make me see that they could make working there miserable for me and encourage me to quit. The supervisors began to display frustration with me for just requesting time off for Terry's appointments. There were people planning pregnancies and taking time off and when they had to work, it was from home. I felt this was intentional stress and undo pressure designed to force me into leaving my job.

They were sending me a clear message that I was not going to get the same treatment as other employees. They wanted to flex their muscles, like a bully who takes payoffs from you when you want to walk down their street without getting beat up. Everybody didn't have to pay, but the underdogs have to pay, whatever rate they set. This was their turf. They set the rules, everybody follow their rules, and yes, some of us paid. A cost that would later prove to have been too great. I had to do what I had to do. Terry was suffering with pain in his chest. He was in need of surgery and I was his confidant, his companion and his care giver. I had to take off work when he had appointments, and I did. I was there for him because I was all he and my children had. They depended on me to be there for them. The supervisors were not happy, and neither was I. The stress of feeling that I might lose my job if I took off for doctor appointments was unbearable. But I had to bear it, it was unavoidable.

I could not possibly think of taking time off from work to take care of pressing financial obligations after having to take time off for medical emergencies. So, I used anytime I had. I prayed and fasted through this time earnestly for Terry's medical condition and our financial position. Things was not supposed to turn out this way. We had recently purchased another home to fit the family just 2 years prior and we were already thinking about refinancing. But this was different, one of us was sick and we had to do it. Everything was due. I was a nervous wreck everything and everybody needed me, so I stayed strong for the other members of the family. Terry was reluctant to stay off work any longer, but he had to take care of this, he could not work. So……as the responsibilities stacked up, I had to carry it. We needed everything, food, clothing, gas, electric, water and shelter. Life has a way of going on. The audacity of life to require that we not only continue to live, but to live at the same economic status through-out our personal financial hardships. Things got real. We believed three things; God would sustain us and if we humbled ourselves under God, He will lift us up in due time. We understood that we could cast our cares upon

God because he cared for us. We were both ministers and we held tight to God's hand.

> ***Psalm 55:22 KJV – Cast thy burden upon the Lord, and he shall sustain thee: he shall never suffer the righteous to be move.***
>
> ***1 Peter 5:6-7 KJV – Humble yourselves, therefore, under mighty hand of God, that he may lift you up in due time. Cast all your anxiety on him because he cares for you.***

We stood on those two scriptures.

Chapter 6
SQUEEZE THE BIG RED PILLOW, WHEN YOU COUGH

IT WAS MARCH OF 2001 WHEN WE WERE called into conference with the surgeon who was referred to us for the open-heart by-pass surgery operation. When we arrived at the office, we were extremely nervous. Terry was not comfortable with the idea that he had to have this surgery. I thought he was acting kind of silly considering the degree of discomfort he was experiencing. He was unable to walk far. He was not back to driving or doing any of his yard work because of the discomfort and distress in his chest cavity. He was taking nitroglycerine like breath mints, and he was barely walking around. Working out in the gym was completely out of the question. He was unable to work, and he was afraid to get too excited because of the tightening he felt in his chest when he did. I was wondering what he was unsure about. He was just not eager with the idea of having surgery. He absolutely did not want to do it. He had this fear that the operation was not going to be successful. I was confident in God and the surgeon. The Lord had been with us through all the previous surgeries, how could he not be with us through the big one. Plus, I was praying and fasting constantly, and I was determined to drag him in there no matter what, God was coming.

In the doctor's office we got a good look at the kind of procedure he wanted to perform, by demonstration of a plastic heart on his desk. What benefits the heart would obtain as a result of the surgery. We were told that death could happen in this kind of surgery, but the odds were small. We didn't have anything to worry about because of the condition Terry's body was in. His age would also work for him. We were assured that he would be fine, his chances were 99 out of 100%. He was in great shape. Terry loved working out everyday if he had time to get there and was feeling well. My husband was still unimpressed. I left the doctors office knowing I would have to do a lot to comfort and reassure him. I was really good at calming Terry's nerves.

We had to do this surgery. We had no other choice. Terry's arteries were clogged again, and nothing could be done about it other than complete replacement. Triple by-pass was the plan. I think the worst part for Terry was having his beautiful chest cracked open. I was not a health and exercise person so I could not understand his attitude of, *I'd rather die,* than upset the well sculptured masterpiece of a body he had worked so hard to build. There was no question in my mind that he had to accept the inevitable and move on down the road to better health. Surely life was more important than a Physique. Could he really be that vain? Or was there something else that terrified him more? He was very quiet though the consultation. I was excited and thrilled that his life could be saved, and he had a *better than good* chance of a full recovery. After all, the doctor did say 99%. So, we agreed to the surgery. We were not really given a choice, just a chance to hear what the surgeon needed to do. We left the office solemnly. For me things were looking up. I always believed that if something could be done to fix any problem and you worked toward getting that done, that things would work out fine, almost like I had a special relationship with life.

Nothing could ever go amuck if I put my hand to it. I could do anything, all I needed was a glimmer of hope and for my sake God would make it happen. Terry was just the opposite. He believed that anything that could go wrong, would go wrong. As it turns out he called this one. This is why the Book of Proverbs advises us to watch what we confess and for 'God's sake' don't teach this kind of unbelief to your children.

> ***In Proverbs 18:20-21 KJV it says,***
>
> ***A man's belly shall be satisfied with the fruit of his mouth; and with the increase of his lips shall he be filled. Death and life are in the power of the tongue: and they that love it shall eat the fruit thereof.***

Matthew Henry's Commentary of the Whole Bible explains the importance of synchronizing your mouth and conscience with what God has declared about our lives and his plans for our lives as believers. In Proverbs 18:20-21

Verse 20 Note, 1. Our comfort depends very much upon the testimony of our own consciences, for us or against us. The belly is here put for the conscience, as Ch. 20:27. Now it is of great consequence to us whether that be satisfied, and what that is filled with, for, accordingly, will our satisfaction be and our inward peace. 2. The testimony of our consciences will be for us, or against us, according as we have or have not governed our tongues well. According as the fruit of the mouth is good or bad, unto iniquity or unto righteousness, so the character of the man is, and consequently the testimony of his conscience concerning him. "We ought to take as great care about the words we speak as we do about the fruit of our trees or the increase of the earth, which we are to eat; for, according as they are wholesome or unwholesome, so will the pleasure or the pain be wherewith we shall be filled." So bishop Patrick. Verse 21 Note, 1. A man may do a great deal of good, or a great deal of hurt, both to others and to himself, according to the use he makes of his tongue. Many a one has been his own death by a foul tongue, or the death of others by a false tongue; and, on the contrary, many a one has saved his own life, or procured the comfort of it, by a prudent gentle tongue, and saved the lives of others by a seasonable testimony or intercession for them. And, if by our words we must be justified or condemned, death and life are, no doubt, in the power of the tongue. Tongues were Aesop's best meat, and his worst. 2. Men's words will be judged of by the affections with which they speak; he that not only speaks aright (which a bad man may do to save his credit or please his company), but loves to speak so, speaks well of choice, and with delight, to him it will be life; and he that not only speaks amiss (which a good man may do through inadvertency), but loves to speak so (Ps. 52:4), to him it will be death. As men love it, they shall eat the fruit of it.

It is vital that we stand guard over our thoughts as to not let evil sayings and thoughts take root so much as to come out of our mouth. I often warned him of such talk.

Terry's surgery was scheduled for the end of July so I went on vacation early in July so that I could have the strength to help him recuperate. He got the operation at the end of July and I remember sitting outside in the waiting room waiting for the operation to end. It seems as if it took forever. He was in the operating room for 7 hours. I was accompanied by my eldest sister, Yvonne and one of Terry's sisters, Paula. I was nervous. Our sisters were making small conversation, insisting that this type of operation was quite common and, in most cases, very successful. I still felt as if something was not quite right. Finally, the surgeon called down to the desk and told me that the operation was a success, but Terry would not be awake for a few hours. I was satisfied with hearing that, so we went out to eat across the street to this little Indian restaurant. A few hours went by and we were allowed to go to the Intensive Care unit to see him, even though he was not awake. I remember that he looked awfully bloated and pale. The doctor explained that all the patients who underwent open heart surgery had a similar grayish complexion and that he would be just fine. Assuring me that his complexion would return to normal from this corpse like appearance and he would lose the water reducing the blotting.

Squeeze The Big Red Pillow, When You Cough

They had him covered with a Postoperative Blanket which was from head to toe.

This was all a part of the open-heart surgery recovery. He would survive. As long as the operation was a success and he was alright, I was alright. He awakened about 3 hour later. Still tired, I spoke to him and left the hospital for the night. I returned on the next day and he was still recovering, after three days he was transferred to the step-down unit. In this unit you're still receiving intensive care, but you are slightly down graded. They allowed him to stay in ICU a day longer than was the routine for this type of surgery because he was running a slight temp. After spending a couple of days in this unit he was transferred to a regular hospital room. His room was filled with other open-heart surgery patients, all male. They were all anxious to be released. They all processed these red heart shape pillows which they were given to squeeze when they had to cough. After a short conversation with some of his roommates I discover some second timers. I found it hard to believe that anybody could stand to go through this surgery twice. But you learn something new every day and that day was no different. There were the second time people and there were other people who belonged to the Third Open Heart Surgery Club. I could not believe what I was hearing, the new arteries could and often do become clogged. Wow, what a traumatic and devastating experience to endure multiple open-heart surgeries. I remember thinking that life just was not fair for some people. I also thought that they must not be changing their lifestyles which had to be contributing to this tragic and desperate attempt at gaining a few more years to live the way they chose to. What a lazy and gluttonous way to live, *eat, drink and be merry for tomorrow we die...* and then to suffer such an extremely dangerous surgery to rectify the damage you have done to yourself. I thought how tremendously sad. What would drive you to want to kill yourself? And then I thought of a statement from 'As a Man Thinketh' by James Allen which reads as such " *Man is made and unmade by himself; in the armory of thought he forges the weapons by which he destroys himself; he also fashions the tools with which he builds for himself heavenly mansions of joy and strength and peace. By the right choice and true application of thought, man ascends to the divine perfection; by the abuse and wrong application of thought, he descends below the levels of beast. Between these two extremes are all the grades of character, and a man is their maker and their master".* What could a person be thinking that would cause his body to continuously remain in the state of fighting against itself. Then I thought *they were probably thinking the same thing my husband is thinking. That he can eat and drink anything he wants, and still be able to govern the effect that the food will have on **his** body. What power could food or drink have over **him**? He is a man, and the laws of nature did not affect him. Stress, what was stress anyway? A man has to do what a man has to do.* Not Good. The wrong thought. Now they were all here, in the same room, hoping that someone else could fix what they played a part in breaking. I quickly dismissed that thought because I realized that it would only discourage me from being my good ole' (*I'm going to help nurse you back to health)* self. He really needed me now.

Terry stayed in the hospital about six days and then it was back to the ranch. I was a little leery about him coming home because the right leg calf where one of the arteries had been harvested from was still draining quite a bit. I was anxious about having the thought of having to clean the wound. It measured at least 4 inches long and 1 inch deep. We left the hospital with bandages, prescriptions, lots of instructions and a big red heart shaped pillow for Terry to squeeze when he coughed.

I was apprehensive about taking him home because he was still running a temperature. Terry insisted on going home.

Chapter 7
A Friend In Your Need Is A Friend Indeed

When I returned to work, I found out that my accounts had been having problems and I immediately jumped right into the madness. Trying to compensate for what had been a very intense and emotional six or so days. I was on the phone with the site straightening out the problems that they were experiencing. I loved my work. I loved helping people with service issues. I love the mystery of the hardware and software problems that arose. I prided myself in the fact that I was an adept troubleshooter. Troubleshooting was a challenge to me. I had 17 years of field service experience and there were not many problems that I was lost on. I would become deeply absorbed in my work when I was at work. I just loved what I was doing. When I returned, I quickly picked up where I left off. I was a natural at fixing computer networks and systems problems. Upon returning to work I realized that I was facing the same issues with the work environment that I had before vacation and Terry's operation. I made a conscience decision to watch my back, before I find myself pulling a dagger out of it. The air was thick everyday. I was nervous at work, afraid to make a mistake, like going to the ladies' room and forgetting to log-out of the queue. Like getting to work two minutes late. Like returning back from lunch a few minutes late. I became very paranoid. Every time I left my desk, I looked for signs that someone had been snooping around it. I took everything that was personal and private home. Everyday I looked for little indications that they were monitoring me, trying to avoid the land mines. I knew that one wrong step would be my last. I literately began to look at my tires and under my car after work. Everything and everyone became suspect. My family and friends must have thought I was insane. I tried not to discuss this with just anyone, especially the other people at work. I kind of thought like a criminal, the less people I associated with, the less people they would target. I realized at this point that I didn't want to pull anyone else into the line of fire. They had families and they did not deserve to go down like this. So, God sent me someone else I could go out to lunch with and cry on her shoulder, and she turned out to be an excellent listener. Most of the time she laughed at what I thought was going on. I became increasingly anxious and insistent about not walking out of range and being unable to return to work on time. She was patient with me. She thought that I could not be serious because we worked for the same company in different divisions and nobody, but nobody had to ever watch the clock at lunch hour. To her this was my imagination working overtime birthed out of anxiety. But if I had to be back, she would have me back because she was my friend. I confided in her because I could trust her. She never told anyone anything I said about what I was experiencing. At the time I had no idea how much I would rely on her friendship and her attentive ear. Sometimes she would get angry about what I said was going on in that center. Demanding that I react to the treatment. Her desk was right outside the door. And that's exactly where I needed her to sit. She would see me step out of the door and by the look in my eyes, she could tell when I needed to vent. Most of our lunch hours turned into Psychotherapy sessions for both of us. But mainly for me. She had a way of welcoming the spillage. I tried to be attentive to her needs also. She always appreciated what I had to contribute to her dilemmas. I was 10yrs her senior and had already been though most of the events she was going though. They all seemed so small to me. Sometimes I would think to myself (*if that was all I had to worry about, I would be blessed*). So many days I had so much to say, but who was I to even think my problems were greater than anybody else's. Every person believes his issues are the more important issues, in view of the mere fact, that they are his. We are all so vain. It becomes a sacrifice for us to restrain ourselves from the impulse to self detonate just long enough to entertain the idea that some one else may feel less constrained to do so. Publilius Syrus said, "He knows not when to be silent who knows not when to speak". How true the saying. Timing and understanding is everything. Matters are commenced with timing and understanding, and they are also concluded with them. This friendship blossomed in such a divinely calculated season; it could not have been planned. With her courage to be seen with me at work long enough to listen to me, I could get through this.

Chapter 8
Trouble Brewing

Shortly upon arrival home from the hospital I noticed that the incision made in surgery by the harvesting of his right leg calf artery was still draining quite a bit. The hospital had a service that provided visiting nurses to our home to monitor his recovery. I was really appreciative for the service. I could not take off from work because of our financial disposition. I asked my supervisor if they could allow me to work from home for awhile. I could see that Terry needed me at home and I dreaded leaving him home alone. The answer was no. There were people in our department who were afforded the opportunity, but I was not one of them. They began suggesting that I take a sick leave without pay. For me that was not an option. I explained that I could not afford that privilege. I went to work and came home everyday to change bandages and clean wounds. Terry was beginning to complain about having strange dreams which included people visiting us, running around in the back yard, who had human bodies and Rooster heads. I contacted the cardiologist and he said that it sounds as if he was a having a reaction to the anesthesia used during surgery. He would get over this shortly. Within the next couple days, he began to have chills, this was the second week out of the hospital, and I began to worry. He was still having delusions and frightening dreams. He was having chills not to mention that there still appeared to be a hole in his chest that had not closed up, which was oozing this yellow puss like substance. The first week he was seen by his doctor and looked fine to the doctors at the office. The second week the drainage began to turn green and become thicker and I became unable to keep the wound clean or dry. Within 2 minutes the bandages had to be replaced on the wound again. I called the Doctors office. The doctor wanted to see him again because of the symptoms he was experiencing. The worst part was taking the day off from work again to take him back to the doctor's office. I literately hated asking my bosses for time off at this point. But this could not wait, even if I lost my job. We arrived at the doctor's office and waited patiently to be seen. When it was our turn Terry nervously joked with the nurses. He was asked to disrobe. The physicians on duty came in to have a look. The gauze covering the wound was full of the substance. The physicians lanced the incision that was made during the surgery to have a closer look. After having a look, they took cultures. We received some Cipro and a comment from the doctor that went something like this, "This medication will either take care of it or cause it to grow worst". We headed home with the medication, and instructions to fill the incision with saline solution and pack it with gauze twice a day. A nurse would drop by the house for a few days to check the wound, but I must clean it myself. I was not comfortable with this because the incision was at lease 2 inches long and an inch deep. They lanced down to the wire protruding from the chest bone, it simply looked disgusting to me. This was Tuesday. I went back to work on the following day, reluctantly. I was informed by one of the supervisors that had assigned himself to *the watch Joanne project* and that I was using the phone for personal reasons more than other people and that this had to stop. I explained that if I could not be home, I must call to make sure my husband was doing alright because his condition might be taking a *not so good* turn. I was met with the comment, "We all have similar problems and families to worry about." At that very moment, if I thought I may be imagining their malicious treatment towards me because of events that had preceded this illness, his comment erased all doubt. Everyone else called whomever they wanted and talked as long as they wanted and discussed whatever they wanted to. I should know, considering I was among the people who filled in for people while they talked. This to me was cruel. I thought that this pressure could be aimed at me to cause me to take off, but without pay. I could not do it. The nurse met me at home in the evening to see the wound. I protested having to do this, it made me literally sick to my stomach, but I was careful to hide my squeamishness from my husband because from where he sat, he could not see it. He had no idea of how it looked. I did not want to alarm him. After two days the incision looked worst to me and I confronted the nurse. She assured me that everything was fine, but I was concerned. I would clean the wound and give medicine in the morning. Terry was able to prepare his own meals and then I would redress the wound in the evening. On Friday morning Terry took a shower and but I happen to catch a glimpse of the bandage in the early morning, it was drenched in puss. He hopped in the shower and I cleaned the wound out with saline and put a clean bandage on it. I dreaded going in to work that day, this meant that I had to call the doctor and report what I was seeing and there was a possibility that I would have to leave work. Then the worst part for me was asking for permission to leave. The prospect of asking for more time off terrified me. But I had to call the doctor. When I called Terry's surgeon, he wanted us to come in for X-rays and another examination. I had to ask. I went into work. When I asked, they told me that I would not be getting paid for anymore time off. All my time had run out and I would not be allowed to leave work this way again. I began to cry right there in front of my bosses. I was embarrassed but I was at the point of breaking under the stress. I told them that I would call them back to let them know if I decide to go out for 8 weeks without pay. Why were they doing this to me? Why couldn't they see that I was in a dilemma and I needed mercy? They had accommodated many others before me with less urgent situations to attend to, why? I was sure of their intentions and plans for me after that transpired. Couldn't we just put the past behind us for a moment? Why couldn't they see that we were fighting against much bigger demon? I thought, if they allowed me to get through with this issue, I can handle whatever they had to threw at me?

I drove back to my hometown which was 25 miles east of my job to pick up my husband. We then drove 50 miles in the opposite direction, west to the doctor's office which included a lab in the building. We were across from the hospital.

The doctor ordered X-rays and blood work for us and then he did a physical exam. We then waited for the X-rays to be developed. It felt like we were literately standing still in time. The sun stood in the same place for what seem like hours. We were nervous. Terry wasn't feeling good physically or spiritually. We held hands and waited and prayed and waited and prayed. What were we praying for? We had no idea, but God knew. All we knew was that we were getting some extra attention from the staff. But they were cool beans with what they were discovering. Finally, the surgeon called us into his office and informed us of the fact that there was an infection. It appeared to be around the wired stitches in the sternum. We were instructed to go over to the hospital for admittance, so that the Infectious Disease doctor could examine the incision and treat the infection. We were made aware of the fact that the surgeon assigned to go into the chest cavity to clean up the infection may have to move over Terry's right pectoral muscle to cover the heart after the job of cleaning is done while in surgery. The Surgeon who had performed the initial surgery was going on vacation. That in itself made us uneasy. Terry immediately began to cry. He understood exactly what was happening and he had this eerie feeling that this surgery might go terribly wrong for him. He had called it. We waited at the doctor's office until we both gathered our composure enough to ask for permission to go out to lunch. When the surgeon left the examining room, Terry made what I thought was a strange comment. He made this statement, 'Well, I guess I will go and have my last meal." I encouraged him not to be so negative. The surgeon gave us the go ahead. We just wanted to go to the car and cry some more. We wanted to get our plan of action down pact again in case we had to implement it. When we arrived at our car Terry grabbed a clean t-shirt that was bought along for the trip to change into, covered his face with it, and just cried aloud and openly. We were still parked where people could see us. I was shocked. He was not a man that showed weakness in any form or fashion. He had been so strong though all the angioplasties and angiograms. I had never witnessed such a meltdown from him ever. I thought he might be overreacting a little. We had already been though so much. After all, the operation was only scheduled to be for one hour. We would be in and out. We drove down to a restaurant for lunch and he ordered his favorite food. Fried chicken, mashed potatoes and corn on the cob. I ate silently in order to get our meals to go down smoothly without just busting out and crying. Me for his condition and he for what he thought would be my situation after surgery. It really had not hit me as to what this all meant, for him or me. But for some strange reason Terry perceived that life as we knew it, would change. We then rushed down to the pharmacy to get some sugarless candy and reading literature for the hospital stay. We had no idea what was before us.

We arrived at the hospital that Friday evening feeling a little better. We needed to make ourselves believe that what Terry was feeling, which was his old, 'whatever can go wrong, will go wrong" attitude was off this time. So, we joked at the hospital. We tried to will this 'Bad Omen' feeling away. The Infectious Disease Specialist left Terry's bedside upon gathering his cultures. He left us with the hope and faith that he had the medical aptitude for this job. His statement to us was, "I have access to the latest medical technology that will enable me to identify the strain of infection quickly. It is embedded in the chest cavity and I will treat it before it gets the best of Terry." According to him, "We could whip this thing."

Terry beckoned me over to sit on his bed with him and talk. So, I slid in beside him. Terry was always joking around, especially at times like this to break the tension in the air. First, we laughed at the receptionist at the physician's office who saw him in the hat he was now wearing and began to hum the theme song for Gilligan's Island. We laughed because before that incident Terry loved sporting that hat. He had purchased it in Montauk while on vacation one year. He was now trying it on my head. Terry than began to sing a song called 'Patches' to me. The lyrics to the song went something like this, *'Patches, I'm dependin' on you, son I've tried to do my best, it's up to you to do the rest.'* This song was about a father who was dying, and he was leaving his last instructions for his son to care for the family from that day on. He was actually transferring the responsibility for the family to the next person in the household. I quickly dismissed the notion that he was going to die and drove home for the night. I promised him that I would be at the hospital bright and early in the morning for the operation. I had never not been present before and after for any of his surgeries. I was always there to assure him that everything would go well and pray with him. Terry was such a baby when it came to me leaving him especially at the hospital.

The next morning, I awoke early and took the children to my Aunt Molly's home for the day. She had agreed to watch them for me. There was a

Country Fair going on around her block and we both thought it would take their minds off where I was going. Her house was located near the center of the fair. The family joined her every year. Plus, grandma would be staying for some extra support.

With Terry's shaving bag in hand. I rushed to the hospital to catch him before surgery.

When I stepped off the elevator on the third floor the doors opened at the Nurses' Station. There was a doctor standing behind the desk speaking with the nurses. I thought it odd that he would have his surgical gear, mask, lab coat and gloves on behind the desk at the Nurses' Station. I saw small splats of blood on his clothes. Then I noticed that they were whispering, and I heard the nurse tell him, "There is Mrs. Humbles now." The surgeon calmly pulled down his mask and walked towards me, to introduce himself. I cannot adequately describe the horrible feeling I got in the pit of my stomach at that moment to this very day. He escorted me to a side conference room, and he asked me to sit down please. I sat down and he sat across from me in a chair facing me. He began with, "I'm sorry to inform you that Terrance is going to die." He went on to explain that he had no way of knowing how bad the infection was before he opened the chest cavity. The X-rays had not revealed the extent of the infection. When he opened the chest cavity the sternum was rotten, he saw that an artery had disconnected itself from the heart and attached itself to the back-wall lining, he cut the artery to reattach it to the heart and was unable to stop the bleeding. He had to actually amputate the artery. Terry had suffered a lack of blood to the brain for at least 20 minutes. His heart had been on a cooling machine for well over the recommended safe standard of time allotted for the cooling of any heart. An extra hour to be exact. He had come out of surgery to tell me that Terry was bleeding, and he could not stop him. I needed to call the immediate family in and prepare the Undertaker of my choice to pick up the body. He was sure that Terry would not live. His condition was grave, and he would not make it through the night. I was floored. I said to the doctor that this man was only 43yrs old. How could this be happening? He told me that he would help me in any way he could. I was in shock. I went on rambling about how I was in litigation with his job for

Workman's Compensation and was due to appear in court tomorrow morning for the purpose of payment for the hospital. I just did not know what to do. He offered me his office to make phone calls out to the family. First, I ran outside and called his sister and I could not reach her. I definitely did not want the doctor to tell me he was deceased while I was all alone at the hospital. I didn't know what to do. Then I called my own sister, she was not available either. Terry had made me promise to not tell his family about the operation before-hand because he didn't want to upset them. I walked back up to the floor where the office was and that's when I saw my own sister, Yvonne, walking down the hall towards me. I have never in my whole life been so relieved to see a familiar face. I must have looked petrified to her. She asked me what was going on? I told her that Terry was not going to live, and I asked her to step into the office with me to call the rest of the family. I was so distraught that she took over the calling. She was so strong that day, it seems that she just suddenly acquired strength. I know that God was there with us because she was always saying that she didn't think she would be able to hear bad news standing up on two feet anyway. She always asked me how I was able to do it. Today, she was a Pillar of Strength. When the doctors came out of surgery, they explained that they had closed Terry up, but before that they had cleaned out the chest cavity the best they could. They had scrubbed the heart off, for it had been completely covered in infection. They seem to be presenting us a little bit of hope. They took a 'Let's wait and see attitude'. My sister wanted to talk about nurses for him for his home care, but the doctors didn't want to go that route. They were just hoping that by the grace of God, he might make it through the night. His condition was grave. I was just devastated. He was too young for this. Terry had called this one, less than twenty-four hour ago, he had had a feeling that things would turn fatal.

Chapter 9
HIS GRACE IS SUFFICIENT

I WAITED FOR THE REST OF THE FAMILY TO arrive. All of this seemed so unfair. How could this happen to our family? How would I tell the children? They had no idea the operation would be so serious. How could I tell them that their vibrant, Weightlifting Coach/Personal Trainer, Recreation Coordinator and overall health buff father was dead. He had always made so light of his sickness. He still had muscles in there lying on that gurney. His body had no time to even physically change. He was not supposed to be dead and... strong. How could this be?

I made a Saturday midday call to one of the supervisors to let him know that things had gone terribly wrong and that I would keep him posted, but we were expecting Terry to die any minute now. He was nervous, *he must have been thinking that he regretted thinking that my issues with Terry was like everyone else's issues. Evidently, they turned out to be a little more pressing. I was angry with him. He had pressed me, and he was winning. Was he happy now? My husband was dying tonight then maybe I could serve him better. We were probably thinking the same thoughts. If I had not been under scrutiny at work, I would have taken a chance and stayed home with my husband anyway. I was aware of the discharge and I was aware of the fact that things was not going quite as smoothly with the recovery process as I had hoped. There was a non-spoken oath between us now. Some of this was his fault. I wasn't going to take all the blame for this. He had been a factor. A big factor. I was afraid of his gigantic God like ego. He could fire me, or he could pressure me into leaving. He knew that I would either cave, or this was all out WAR.*

After speaking with him, I called Terry's job and told them the story. They gave me their sympathies. I felt as if I needed to justify why Terry felt he was too sick to return to work. I felt as if I wanted to crawl out of my skin. Skin was uncomfortable right now. I felt a responsibility to justify our feelings and guilt for everything that had transpired. There was no real reason for me to feel these emotions, but I did.

How could Terry tell me not to tell his family? Now what was I supposed to tell them? That he had an emergency operation and during the operation he died...? That seemed so cruel to me. And it seemed even crueler that he would leave me here to face their questions and inquisitions. My idea was to tell them because if something goes wrong, I wouldn't be cold calling. And here I was cold calling, pushed to the front line again. I was angry, But Terry's feeling about his sickness and his Right to Privacy was personal and I had to respect his wishes. This was a very hard thing for me to do. Why would you not want people to know? Most people pray and prepare when one of their loved ones go into surgery. WHY... I could not understand him. I did as he asked me to do. This was his decision. None of them had time to say anything that they might have wanted to say to him before this happened. They must have felt so cheated. We came from two completely different worlds. My family, sisters, brothers, aunts, uncles, cousins call each other for everything. I guess, we're all kind of selfish, when it comes to expecting and welcoming a lot of support from each other. This has always served us well in cementing the family closer together in the time of crisis. All axes are laid down, when a member of the family has a crisis. The crisis is always on the front burner. It is automatically transformed into a family crisis. Everybody responds and nobody is exempt. I guess that's where our Indian heritage comes in at. If you have nothing to give in word or deed you just sit with the injured party. But people are different, he had his reasons. That is one of the more important roles that makes us excellent caregiver. You must respect the wishes of the patient, because after all, these are the patients wishes. You may feel differently but you must not violate the patients right to his personal privacy. And it's a very thin line between violation of that right, and your wishes disguised, all dressed up as good intentions. With chronically or terminally ill patients there will be so many other chances to make decisions. You must know what decisions are important to the patient and show them consideration by respecting their Right to Choose. What may be important to you may not be important to the patient and vise verse. People are all different, regardless of how well you think you know them. When the rubber meets the road, you will find some new uniqueness that might have not been displayed to you in the past. They have to trust you to respect who they are, and not take advantage of their situation for selfish or egotistic reasons. Go with it. Allow the patient the right to take off the mask.

We then formed a prayer chain. I called my church and they called their prayer affiliates. Everyone that came to the hospital and those who we knew but who couldn't come, did the same. There were churches and ministers throughout the united states praying for a miracle. We were praying that God would let Terry live through the night. We tried to make all kind of personal deals with God that day. I personally was too weak to pray. I just sat in the waiting room trying to have the strength to bear this lot that I had to handle. Other members of our party prayed for us. I was so weak; it was literately the finger of God that held me up.

The night fell and that was rough for me. Terry had been in this coma for about twelve hours already and he was not stable. I did not want night to come.

I guess I thought if it did, it would be Terry's last night. I dreaded each hour. I couldn't call anyone else. Who else could I tell? Who could fix this? All through the night I remember sneaking away to the ladies' room for a cry or whisper another prayer. Just me talking to God. Maybe he would hear me. If I tried to communicate with him anyway. The pain in my soul was so intense I thought I could not bear it. When I was around others I could not talk, out of fear they would sense my sorrow, or I would break down and cry. How could he leave me a widow at forty-two? We weren't old and ready to retire. We were still young. This was strange, but then I thought, 'some widows were younger than me.' What did they find to do with themselves? How do you adjust to being one person, there were always two of us? What about his friends? A part of my identity resided in being Terry's wife. All of a sudden, I am alone. There is no longer two opinions when making decisions, just me. No one to blame if things go wrong, just me. Can I handle all of this responsibility? I have to handle it. Nobody was as concerned about these issues as me, they were our issues. Nobody's business but mine. Can't bounce anything else off Terry. He thought

I never took his advice seriously, just like every other husband in the world thinks, but I always took him seriously. After all he only used the side of his brain that was used for logic. Emotions were always a problem for me when I made decisions. I didn't always use all of his advice, but I considered it. His logic mixed with a bit of Mom's emotion would always win out. What good was scolding the kids anyway without adding a tear or two. If I had to have some drama, everybody got drama. That's what made me mom, and not dad. But then what would I do without dad? Who would listen to me and say, "It'll be fine sweetheart, just move from in front of the TV for a minute?" Who would be able to have the patience with me that dad had? He saw through my strong façade and he under girded me, never reprimanding me. When I couldn't lift the weights that I was trying to lift, he would just spot me. Being careful to not let me strain under the load or drop them on my chest. What would I do now? The pain of loosing a spouse is excruciating.

About 7 o'clock pm I bumped into the doctor in the elevator on the way down from the Intensive

Care Unit and he said that frankly he was surprised that Terry was still hanging on.

Through the night I slept fitfully in the front lobby of the hospital checking in hourly to see how Terry was doing with the Third-Floor Nursing Station. They informed me that the doctor's rounds were at 7 o'clock every morning at which I could obtain a full report. I was there at 7:00am. The doctor told me that he had experienced some seizures during the night and had received medication to control it. He was pleased to see that Terry was still with us. The following day would be busy for him. Tests were ordered, CAT scan, EEG, MRI and the such. They were studying his brain activity.

The family held a hospital vigil for the next few days. Hostility and tension filled the room. Days of it, that felt like weeks.

> *People respond to tragedy in their own personal ways. Some people become uncommunicative, some talkative, some protective, some embittered, some inquisitive, some*

defensive, some indignant, some regretful, some struggle with guilt and some are grateful and reflective. They deal with a collogue of emotions and psychological mental attitudes. The wise reaction is to display humility and strive to consider and respect those in your present company when you react. Try to understand that everyone is under the stress of dealing with the same dilemma you are faced with. Try to imagine yourself in their shoes, this will assist you in putting things into perspective. It is very difficult for all persons involved. They are just as distressed and distraught as you are. Some individuals are more. Most people don't express outwardly what they feel inwardly. Their feelings will remain a secret until you violate them. You will know when you have crossed that invisible but definitely distinct line in the sand.

Three days passed and Terry was still alive. He crossed his legs and his body jerked involuntarily. The doctor told us that he was not aware of his actions, but we wanted to believe he was in control of all of them. On the third day I left the hospital with a good friend who insisted on taking me home to change my clothes and allow me a shower. When I got back home, I picked up the children and explained the multiple complications. They were devastated, and in shock. I explained that the physician had little hope that Terry was going to live. I took my daughter to the side to talk to her personally as she was exceptionally close to her father. She was only six years old. We held each other and cried together. I took my shower, changed my clothes and my girl friend drove me back to the hospital. On the way, we dropped the children off again at my aunt's home. Faith was left in the care of her older brother and my aunt, her great aunt. They were safe and I was again free to go back to my husband's bedside. On the fourth day Terry's kidneys began to shut down and his body began to fill up with water. At this time the hospital also got my permission to insert a feeding tube into his nose. Terry's tongue began swell and his lips were swelling also. His appearance was almost unbearable. At this point I made a decision that I thought Terry would have made for himself.

I had the hospital stop the visitors. I had no idea that some people would take it personally, but it really was not about them, it was about Terry. The feeding tube was spilling liquid out of the nose and his appearance was not what he would have wanted people to remember about their visit with him. I had to respect him; he would have done the same for me. There is no way he would have wanted visitors to see him in that state. Terry's family began their journeys home. My sister and I stayed at the hospital another two days. On the sixth day Terry's doctor broke the news to me that he thought that Terry would come out of the coma in a few days. The only problem was that if he did not "awaken properly" that they would have to put him down again. According to the physician to not "awaken properly" meant that if he awakes and is not in his right state of mind, he would be have to be sedated again. I was so happy to hear this great news that I could hardly contain myself from the joy that was flooding my soul. I went home to sleep in my own bed at this point and I needed to pick up the kids too. The doctors began to work on the kidney problems and Terry began to get rid of the water that he was retaining. On the ninth day, Monday before Terry was to awake, his doctor call me in to give me the results from his test. His assessment of the damage. We met at about 7:00pm in the evening. As we sat across from each other I felt that whatever I was about to hear was going to be welcome. All I knew was that Terry was going to live and I could handle anything but losing Terry. He began by saying that Terry's condition was stabilized, and they were expecting him to awaken soon. He then began to tell me that the testing showed that Terry had suffered Frontal Lobe Brain Damage. He also had suffered additional injuries to the heart. A bundle was preformed to close the heart on the right side as a result of having to remove an artery that transported blood to the brain. The doctor told me that if he lives, he would be a vegetable for the rest of his life. All of this went right over my head. I don't know if it was because I was happy because he was going to live or if I was so tired and worn out from the whole ordeal. I took this opportunity to return home for a shower. I wanted to tell the children about this miracle. I decided to continue to return to the hospital each morning, and then on the second day out, I was vacuuming the house before heading back when a praise that I had not known was possible, came straight up out of my soul. The Lord then spoke to me saying, *"If you don't praise me even the rocks will cry out."* Then He spoke these words to me, "I will raise Him up today." I realized at that very moment that God could praise himself without priming the pump, as they say. Before then I always believed that we have to make an effort to praise Him. I thought we had to encourage ourselves to produce a praise unto Him. I discovered that God can compel and control all of your being to praise Him, as with the rocks. He can make good on his promise.

> ***Luke 19:40 NKJV****, Jesus tells us, "But He answered and said to them, "I tell you that if these should keep silent, the stones would immediately cry out."*

I quickly put everything away and rushed to the hospital. When I arrived, he was out of ICU and in a recovery room. I walked up to him and he immediately opened his eyes. He opened his eyes for the first time in 10 days and he was inside of his body. During the coma his eyes were opened at times but there was no soul inside his body. Terry was back and present. Smiling and pleased to see me. He was unable to talk but I was anxious to know where he had been and what he had seen. The question came out so fast, "Where have you been? Have you been to Heaven?". He shook his head yes... "Have you seen Jesus? Has he talked to you?" He shook his head yes with a full dreamy look in his eyes. I had the doctor take the breathing tube out of his throat. I expected that he would spew out the whole story, but he couldn't speak. For the next week I would be swabbing his mouth in the morning and suctioning saliva out of his throat as the feeding tubes were still inserted into his nose. Terry began to insist that I bring the children up to see him. I had been reluctant because he didn't appear to be mentally stable. Crying, having out bursts and refusing to willingly let me leave the hospital at night, displaying textbook 9-year-old behavior. He was left with the common physical conditions experienced after a stroke and Traumatic Brain Damage. I was afraid to bring

Faith up to the hospital because she was only six and unable to understand why he appeared to be so different. He had been rendered officially mentally impaired by the asphyxiation he had experienced in surgery. Because of his insistence I drove the kids up to visit, I prepared them by talking to them about his condition. My son understood as he was a freshman in college, but Faith was terrified with this new man. They were so close before the operation, he did everything for her and with her. I quickly cut their visit short and transported the children home.

Chapter 10
It's A Long Way Home

I had not at this point completely researched what having Frontal Lobe Brain Damage meant, but I would soon find out... It was surely nothing to take lightly. I was ecstatic just to think he was on the road to recovery. A massive upgraded from dying. The first job was to deal with his feeding tube. We had problems with his feeding tube from the beginning. It kept becoming sucked back into the stomach cavity. Every few days he had to have it surgically pulled back out again. This meant X-rays to find it and a small surgical procedure to fish it out. What a headache. He also had an Intravenous (IV) Central Line placed into his vein for the massive amounts of antibiotics being administered for the staph infection, which the hospital was yet uncertain regarding its strain. Terry could not walk or talk. Seeing him in this condition was the hardest thing I ever had to do. He had to learn to walk and talk again. After two days on the step downward he began to have tremors that was so violent that he could not stand up on his feet. The staff had problems getting him from the chair to the bed. It took four of the staff. He was a big guy. He had suffered Traumatic Brain Injury... In a few days he began to try to communicate with me. He was puzzled about the fact that he could understand me, but I could not understand him. He wanted to know what had transpired in the operation. He knew something was wrong. I was able to understand everything he tried to say. Its amazing to think that God would provide everything you need regardless of the condition in which you find yourself. But this is exactly what God does. He certainly and unquestionably filled our needs. The needs that we are aware of and those that we are unaware of ever existing. We only posses the capacity to ask for what we think we need. God sees everything and while we wrestle with the obvious, he tackles the unseen and the unforeseen. We could not possibly handle everything that is going on at one time, it would literately destroy us, emotionally and physically. So, God handles our business without us. It may concern us, but it is prevented from overtaking us. The nurses in the Step-Down Unit gave excellent care. They gave us both, all they had to give. Terry was totally confused and struggling desperately to regain his former state of being. I really don't believe he was able to accept what had happened to him. Weeks passed with much Physical Therapy and changes in medication, as well as, his condition. All the changes were not necessarily good ones. He developed other conditions as a result of the antibiotics and neurological medications. The hospital suggested after about 3 weeks that he be transferred to a Traumatic Brain Injury Rehabilitation Center. The hospital's Social Worker and I began the process of searching for the one that would best serve his needs. We found one that was only 35 minutes away from our home. Terry was not pleased having to be transported to another facility, but he still had an intravenous main line for antibiotic administration, and a feeding tube inserted into his body. That was when I began to realize he might never be the same again. He seemed very immature and child like in his demands. He was totally unable to help himself do anything. He was given Speech Therapy and taught to use his throat again, and slowly began to become able to swallow baby food. The feeding tube was removed from his stomach. Every bit of progress he made, we celebrated. I believed that he would recover fully. When I took him home, he was still very sick. I recall being so afraid driving home with him. But I was it. I was all he had. Nobody else would consider taking him home. I was to come to the realization in the months ahead that we lost Terry on the operating table. The Terry I once knew, anyway. Looking back, I am sure people must have thought I was foolish for not placing him in a residence wherein professional people could care for him. At that time, I would not consider that idea. I dismissed it. He was going to come back 100%. Who can say what will transpire in another person's health or life for that matter? With that, I took the challenge. Terry was only 44yrs old, how could his life be over. He was up for the adventure. I'm sure he also believed that if he could only get home to the kids and the gym, he would fully recover. The next few weeks was busy with Physical Therapy, Occupational Therapy, Speech Therapy, Doctor visits and Nursing Home visits. With all of this, we were finding that Terry still experienced pain in his right leg, so excruciating that he could hardly walk. This was the leg that some of the arteries were harvested from and used for bypass surgery on his heart. We suspected that there was something still wrong.

Chapter 11
He Was Caught Up To Meet Him

Upon returning safely home, it was my time to get all the facts about Heaven out of Terry. Terry could talk and walk again. I was patiently awaiting the day when he was able to articulate to me the details of Heaven and all the facts about Jesus. Every day I found the opportunity to set with Terry and reiterate the facts while pulling more facts out of him about his experience.

Here is his story. Mind you, every time he talked about it, he cried because he was missing the presence of Jesus Christ. Oh how... he wished he had been allowed to stay with him. Heaven was Heavenly. He told me when he awaken that he was standing on a dock. The water was a deep aqua blue color. This proves to us that the moment that we are absent in the body, deceased, we will appear instantly before the Lord, as Apostle Paul says in:

2 Corinthians 5:6-10 KJV,

Therefore we are always confident, knowing that, whilst we are at home in the body, we are absent from the Lord: (For we walk by faith, not by sight:) We are confident, I say, and willing rather to be absent from the body, and to be present with the Lord. Wherefore we labour, that, whether present or absent, we may be accepted of him. For we must all appear before the judgment seat of Christ; that everyone may receive the things done in his body, according to that he hath done, whether it be good or bad"

In other words, we are confidently walking encouraged by our faith, although we know that while we are present in our in the body, we are away from the Lord. We likewise would prefer to be away from our bodies and at home with the Lord in Heaven. So, we desire to please Him, whether we dwell here in this body or are away from it. For we must all appear before the judgment seat of Christ, that each of us may receive our just due for the things that we have done in the body, whether good or bad.

The waters were calm and very still, but they were bright deep aqua blue. *As a matter of fact, all the colors in Heaven were alive, not like the dull dead colors we experience here on earth. They were living breathing entities.* While he stood on the dock, a stream of points of lights were pointing him to where Jesus was. He looked down and a boat was there at the dock. He saw that our Brother-In-Law, Craig Neil was in the boat wearing a hat and a pair boots playing his guitar. He asked God, "What was he doing there?" His answer was, "He travels to and fro... between heaven and earth." At the time Craig was a Musician and a Minister for a church located in Harlem, New York. Terry then remember thinking that God had a sense of humor. After which Craig disappeared from the boat. Then Terry got into the boat and paddled out to the midst of the body of water. In the middle of the waters was a large man figure. Only the shoulders of the man was sticking out of the water. The man was huge, and he identified himself as God the Father. The funny thing was, that the man looked just like him. He climbed out of the boat onto the back of the Father and he immediately melted into the body of the figure. He felt completely satisfied, warm and squishy blending into the Father. He felt as if they were one. He heard a loud voice speak to him saying, "Have you met my son Jesus?". Do you know My son Jesus?". Terry said that, "He sounded like many waters." Powerful and commanding, His words were rolling, roaring and echoing from His belly.

Revelation 1:15 NKJV says,

> *"His feet were like fine brass, as if refined in a furnace, and His voice as the sound of many waters".*

He perceived that God was adamant about him getting to know His son Jesus. Terry said that the Father was wearing clothes like his and His body looked just like his, He looked like him.

Genesis 1:26-27 KJV,

"Then God said, "Let Us make man in Our image, after Our likeness, to dominate over the fish of the sea and the birds of the air, over the cattle, and over all the earth itself and every creature that creeping upon it." So, God created man in his own image, in the image of God created he him; male and female created he them."

***1 John 3:2-3 KJV** says,*

"Beloved, we are now children of God, and what we will be has not yet been revealed. We know that when Christ appears, we will be like Him, for we will see Him as He is. And everyone who has this hope in Him purifies himself, just as Christ is pure."

I cannot explain Terry seeing God the Father as appearing to look like himself. I can only tell you what he said to me. All the commentaries describes this scripture as meaning that we will be like God morally and spiritually... Because God is a spirit. It's interesting that with every country that I have visited all of it famous artist that have painted Jesus and his family paints them with their own physical characteristics. If I am in a church or museum in Italy than any portraits of the Virgin Mary and infant Jesus were painted as if their nationality was Italian. We see Jesus as we are, I suppose.

I am very fond of David Guzik's Bible Commentary explanation of it. It includes the perspective of Charles Haddon *Spurgeon*.

We shall be like Him, for we shall see Him as He is:

*John made the connection between seeing **Him as He is** and our transformation to be like Jesus. We can say that the same principle is at work right now. To the extent that you see Jesus **as He is**, to that same extent, you are like Him in your life. We can say that this happens by reflection.*

"When a man looks into a bright mirror, it makes him also bright, for it throws its own light upon his face; and, in a much more wonderful fashion, when we look at Christ, who is all brightness, he throws some of his brightness upon us." (Spurgeon)

Next, Terry found himself back in the rowboat sitting beside Jesus. The love of God was emitting from Jesus and it was so strong Terry carried this feeling and experience to his grave. He came back saying, "If we knew how much Jesus loved us and our brothers and sisters on earth, we would never ever mistreat another person. If we know that Jesus was Himself pure love, we would love ourselves and others the same way. Terry would cry every time he recollected and remembered the love of God. Tears would just pour out of his eyes. Jesus' love would overwhelm him. It was as if he was sitting right there in the presence of God all over again. Jesus showed him images of everything he could desire, money, gold, jewelry, cars, houses, ice cream, cookies and candy as if he was a kid. Jesus not only showed him his desires which all came alive with all his senses attached, he told him that he had everything he wanted and needed in Him and was willing and able to give them to him. He assured him that He had all things in him. His answer is yes to all our desires. The form of communication between he and Jesus was by mental telepathy. Neither of them used speech.

2 Corinthians 1:20 KJV

"For all the promises of God in him are yea, and in him Amen, unto the glory of God by us."

Whatever Jesus wants to do for us, the Father God is saying yes to. The father does not say no to the Son.

Did Jesus have authority to do this? Yes, He did.

Matthew 11:27 KJV says,

"All things are delivered unto me of my Father: and no man knoweth the Son, but the Father; neither knoweth any man the Father, save the Son, and he to whomsoever the Son will reveal him.". Everything that Terry saw in Heaven was backed up by the scripture.

Matthew Henry's Commentary on the Whole Bible explains to us a perfect invitation offered by Jesus to come ... It says,

> "Matthew 1:25-30, It becomes children to be grateful. When we come to God as a Father, we must remember that he is Lord of heaven and earth, which obliges us to come to him with reverence as to the sovereign Lord of all; yet with confidence, as one able to defend us from evil, and to supply us with all good. Our blessed Lord added a remarkable declaration, that the Father had delivered into his hands all power, authority, and judgment. We are indebted to Christ for all the revelation we have of God the Father's will and love, ever since Adam sinned. Our Savior has invited all that labor and are heavy-laden, to come unto him. In some senses all men are so. Worldly men burden

themselves with fruitless cares for wealth and honours; the gay and the sensual labour in pursuit of pleasures; the slave of Satan and his own lusts, is the merest drudge on earth. Those who labour to establish their own righteousness also labour in vain. The convinced sinner is heavy-laden with guilt and terror; and the tempted and afflicted believer has labours and burdens. Christ invites all to come to him for rest to their souls. He alone gives this invitation; men come to him, when, feeling their guilt and misery, and believing his love and power to help, they seek him in fervent prayer. Thus, it is the duty and interest of weary and heavy-laden sinners, to come to Jesus Christ. This is the gospel call; Whoever will, let him come. All who thus come will receive rest as Christ's gift, and obtain peace and comfort in their hearts. But in coming to him they must take his yoke and submit to his authority. They must learn of him all things, as to their comfort and obedience. He accepts the willing servant, however imperfect the services. Here we may find rest for our souls, and here only. Nor need we fear his yoke. His commandments are holy, just, and good. It requires self-denial, and exposes to difficulties, but this is abundantly repaid, even in this world, by inward peace and joy. It is a yoke that is lined with love. So powerful are the assistances he gives us, so suitable the encouragements, and so strong the consolations to be found in the way of duty, that we may truly say, it is a yoke of pleasantness. The way of duty is the way of rest. The truths Christ teaches are such as we may venture our souls upon. Such is the Redeemer's mercy; and why should the laboring and burdened

> **sinner seek for rest from any other quarter? Let us come to him daily, for deliverance from wrath and guilt, from sin and Satan, from all our cares, fears, and sorrows. But forced obedience, far from being easy and light, is a heavy burden. In vain do we draw near to Jesus with our lips, while the heart is far from him. Then come to Jesus to find rest for your souls."**

Terry saw me three times in Heaven. The first thought of me, I turned into a vibrant beautiful living flower full of fragrance and grace. The second time, he observed me writing on the ground with a stick. I was not aware that He and Jesus was standing there with me. He asked Jesus, "What is she doing here? "This is my Prophet; she only does what I tell her to do. Her ministry is a ministry with 'no holds barred" was what he heard. The next time he saw me I was in a big grassy green meadow with the children playing around a picnic table. Jesus told him that if he was to stay in Heaven, I would be well taken care of with the children. The point of the vision was to ease his concern, making him comfortable with what would happen if he choose to keep him in Heaven. Terry then saw a dark horde which looked like a dark rolling cloud placed in the corner on one side of Heaven and he asked Jesus about it. It was a place where he was holding Satan and all his Demons until the time comes for his release on earth. There were also events to come in the future that Terry said he saw and heard while being there that Jesus had forbidden him to speak of.

Revelation 20:1-3 KJV *tells us*

And I saw an angel come down from heaven, having the key of the bottomless pit and a great chain in his hand. And he laid hold on the dragon, that old serpent, which is the Devil, and Satan, and bound him a thousand years, And cast him into the bottomless pit, and shut him up, and set a seal upon him, that he should deceive the nations no more, till the thousand years should be fulfilled: and after that he must be loosed a little season.

Terry then finds himself being bathed in pure white bubbling blinding light in preparation for his return back to his body. He asked Jesus if he could stay in Heaven and the answer was that, "He was not finished on earth, and he must go back." He then woke up in a hospital bed. He had absolutely no remembrance of the surgical procedure. No knowledge of the fact that he had been asleep for 10 days. He was confused about why he was in the hospital.

Chapter 12
KILLING ME SOFTLY

After completing a 2 week of family leave, I returned to work. Upon returning I came back to no changes. As a matter of fact, the employee that passed me the racist joke was still sharing my cubical. I was livid. This inaction made me think that my bosses had absolutely no intention of moving his desk away from me. I immediately e-mailed my personnel director to see if this incident had been reported formally to her. The answer was a telephone conference in the department manager's office with him being present. I was basically told that I was oversensitive because of what I experienced with my husband. I was told that other people had been questioned in response to my accusations of bias treatment within the department and that other people did not feel the same way. I was then told that the joke I received was not offensive to her. She was also the same nationality as me, African American. She said that I was in need of seeking the company's division that helped emotionally disturbed employees. I was deeply upset and agitated with her attitude. She seemed to have her script already prepared for this play. This whole situation threw me. I simply had no idea that personnel would take this position considering the events that had already transpired. I definitely did not expect that no action would be taken following such an incident. Especially after requiring all employees to attend the Company's Sensitivity Seminars. That were specifically designed to increase our awareness and sensitivity concerning our colleagues, with regards to their race, sex, ages or national origin. This was due to a number of hefty lawsuits that were recently awarded due to the violation of civil rights laws in the workplace. I was shaken by what I was hearing. From that moment I felt that I was dead meat. I worked extra hard to do my job. I felt that it would be a matter of time before they conspired to kick me out of the door. Obliviously to management this guy was not their problem, I was. From that very day I knew my days were numbered. Everyone watched me. Absolutely nobody befriended me in my immediate area. They labeled me as the troublemaker. Whistleblowers are unwelcomed in the environment they blow whistles in. I was finished. But I was determined to hold on to my job. I shut my mouth from that point and did all my work. My clients had been visited by another employee and he was allowed privileges that I was not privy to at their work locations. I was never allowed to visit the site of my client. He had gone out to the sites within the 2 weeks that I was out. I had twice the time in the field than this guy and twice the expertise that he had and none of that meant anything. I felt betrayed, and alone, how could I allow myself to get into this situation? Why was I complaining about the treatment of minorities anyway when the other minorities were obviously distancing themselves from me? Betrayed by my bosses, they instructed us to report these incidents only to deny their existence, not to mention their personal involvement in them. Betrayed by my colleagues, they complained to me. We had long extensive conversations about the bias treatment that we received. I trusted that they would not be afraid to talk to management about it and when they all chickened out, my first thought was, I was done.

Chapter 13

Three strikes your'e out!

Just before returning to work Terry was admitted back into the hospital to have a shunt put into his right leg because the doctors had discovered that the artery had narrowed due to scare tissue build up. I felt pressure to not worry about him because I was in danger of losing my job at work. I was the only financial support for the family. I was the sole support, and the children depended on me. I could not lose my job, no... not NOW. I went to visit Terry everyday after work and he was anxious to go home. He had spent so much time in the hospital he was not planning on staying in a moment longer than he had to. I took him home after 4 days and the Physical Therapy started all over. Terry began his journey of rehabilitation but tension on the job was getting worst. My boss called me into a meeting in December and informed me that the company may have some layoffs and if they did that, I would be one of the first to go because of my performance. That's funny, I went from great performance appraisals to unsatisfactory performance appraisals. I felt from the start that this would happen to me in retaliation for whistleblowing. I thought hard and long about what I needed to do. I could not see myself walking away from this company knowing that if I didn't do something about what was going on here, I could not live with myself. Other people would have to suffer the same torture and utter torment that I experienced. This behavior could only be stopped if I had the courage to stand up to my superiors. I could not just put my head in the sand and pretend I had not been violated. Just to think that others would suffer as I had, I could not bear the thought. This was something that was totally unacceptable to me as a human being. If I died trying... I was determined to see policies change, as well as the way issues were handled within the company. I was determined to get the attention of the company as a whole. They understood that they had supervisors in violation of Federal Employment and civil rights laws. And so, on the first of January 2002, I filed a complaint against my employer for racial bias, conspiracy, and retaliation among other charges. The least I could do was help the Company understand that they were breaking Federal Employment Laws and hopefully it would lead to effective company policies becoming implemented that would discourage racial bias behavior. I was determined to change the way this company treated people of color. After filing the Federal law suit the pressure from the staff became so unbearable, I began to withdraw from them. I went to work every day knowing I was being patrolled and scrutinized. I thought they was trying to catch me forgetting to log my telephone out when I left my desk. And with all that I was dealing with, the doctors, hospitals, medicines, the therapies, I am lucky I still have my mind. If I was 1 minute late, I knew things were being documented. I was scared for my very life. I really had to watch my back. The lawsuit was naming 5 bosses who sat right next to me everyday. The company choose this situation as an opportunity to move my department to St. Louis, Missouri. They knew that most of the people named in the lawsuit would not want to move. Hopefully they would trim their fat this way. Everybody hated me for this, and they treated me as such. I was not leaving, I planned to work until the last day before the department closed down.

In the meantime, the Workman's Compensation hearing was in full swing. The doctor from the insurance carrier was arguing the point that they were partially responsible for my husband's condition. And that the hospital caused the permanent damage because they had an accident during surgery causing him to have Frontal Lobe Brain Damage which totally disabled him from returning back to work. Upon hearing the argument, I retained an attorney who investigated the allegations and found this to be true. That's when I commenced to file another lawsuit for Medical Malpractice. All of this was quite overwhelming. I kept my employer informed of everything that was occurring. They took aim and every opportunity to apply pressure. Now I was in three major battles. Workman's Compensation refused to pay for anything without a fight. I paid for medication and doctors visits. The judge ordered them to pay a weekly cash benefit to Terry and all medical expenses. All they did was appeal. Appealing gave them time to delay paying out payments. We spent many weeks without income from Workman's Compensation Administration. I think they thought Terry would either die from his condition or from our inability to obtain medication. The doctors had mercy though, they waited with the bills and continued the treatment. Terry was taking over 20 different pills multiple times a day. My job was helping with medication through my family medical insurance coverage. I was thankful for that. But this too was soon to change. Circumstances would soon call upon the doctors to give us free visits and free medication samples for the next 2 years, which was nothing but a miracle.

This was definitely a time when I felt the hand of God literately hold me up. As we could truly relate to the Apostle Paul's testimony when he suffered trouble in Asia for the sake of the Gospel. He makes this statement in the book of Corinthians:

2 Corinthians 1:8-11 KJV

> *"For we would not, brethren have you ignorant of our trouble which came to us in Asia, that we were pressed*

out of measure, above strength, insomuch that we despaired even of life: But we had the sentence of death in ourselves, that we should not trust in ourselves, but in God which raiseth from the dead: Who delivered us from so great a death, and doth deliver: in whom we trust that he will yet deliver us: Ye also helping together by prayer for us, that for the gift bestowed upon us by the means of many persons thanks may be given by many on our behalf."

I know that the Lord was with us through this time because we struggled tremendously paying for medication without a sufficient income to really do it. Not to mention the physical stress of carrying a family also. He wanted to die, but God kept us. People everywhere who knew us prayed for us. Multiple churches and all of our Christian friends formed prayer circles for us. We were sustained within the eye of this storm. God truly came through for us. We were more able to testify of the greatness of God. Our testimony gave others strength to get through their own struggles while serving God.

This period was particularly hard because we had a son trying to stay in college and a daughter in Catholic School. And our son had recently graduated from Catholic School. Anybody who opts for a private school education for their kids will tell you that it was definitely not easy but completely worth it.

Oh yeah, let's not forget the fact that Grandma was living near us with the onset of Alzheimer's Disease. God gave me the grace and strength to handle everything and not give it a second thought. I believed we could make it with God's help, and we did.

Grandma was so cute during this time. Every time Terry's blood pressure proved to be high, she would insist on hers being taken. She watched him like a big sister taking care of her younger brother. Afraid but brave. When he got sick her mind would tell her to check herself out. Both of them hanging onto my hand. I was the Mother. Terry stole sweets and Mom told on him. We had so many laughs. Grandma was always a prankster. She took great pride in outsmarting everybody. Especially people that were younger than she was. Outsmarting younger people was proof that 'she still had it'. To her it was more fun than doing Crossword Puzzles. She laughed at life itself.

We painted pumpkins on the patio tables every fall with the kids in the back yard. Every Fall without fail we all were together picking out flowers, corn stalks and Indian corn for the front porch. What a sight we must have been, a person from every stage in life together. An elderly 75year old mother (senior), a 43-year-old female, 44-year old male (middle age), an 18-year-old (teenager), and a 6-year-old (little girl). Hormones were flying everywhere and looking back I enjoyed every minute of that life. I made sure we had birthday parties whenever there was a birthday. My patients loved parties. Everybody always came to my home for everything. From Thanksgiving to summer bar-b-ques. We loved entertaining people. We all loved people. Except for the 18-year-old who just wanted to play computer games all night. Blah...

Now as for Terry he was different now, extremely different. When he returned home from the hospital, he was mentally Faith's age, 7. He was equal to her... the baby in the family.

For in a few short years she would age beyond his physical and mental years. She had to care for him as if he was her playmate. He was mischievously eating food that he was forbidden to eat by the doctor. He was putting his coat on inside out and upside down. Stealing cookies from the kitchen. Our relationship went from husband and wife to mother and son. The change was dramatic and devastating to me with absolutely no experience in Traumatic Brain Injury. His favorite pass time became riding to the grocery store to purchase Jell-O when I walked in from work. Often, we would find ourselves back in the nearest emergency room from a sugar reading of nearly 700. Terry had stroke after stroke. His doctor was advising me of his inability to judge what was not good for him to eat. He just wanted to eat and do what he wanted to do as any 9-year-old would. He took his medication when he thought about it. He asked for Cheeseburgers, Ice Cream and Pizza while reaching for chocolate candy at will. Faith, his 7-year-old, made it her business to always rat him out to me. She turned into his older sister. That little one, stayed by my side. She took on a tremendous responsibility as her father's keeper. He pulled rank when he really wanted her to turn a blind eye. It never worked. She always told on him. The risk of not telling on him would hurt her much more than a rebuke from your father.

Chapter 14
INTENSE BATTLES

I WENT FOR SEVERAL MONTHS SUFFERING from the Coodies on the job. Nobody would associate with me on a friendly basis from my department. No open communication with me from the other employees. After all, they felt all of this racial trouble in the department was my fault. Shortly after the announcement regarding the move to sue the company, the fellow who passed around the racist joke sent an intimidating and threatening e-mailed to the group which mentioned buying bullets. I was terrified. The coming months would be very cold... And lonely at work. The air was so intense you could cut the air with a knife. The company decided to move the Customer Response Center to St. Louis, Missouri. People blamed me for the department move. The supervisors worked hard to build *what they thought was* a sure case against me. I filed the lawsuit in March of 2002, and they fired me in November 2002. I had no insurance, no job, and I felt my career was over. I work in a field where ties are close, everyone in my field knows someone that you know. I was not expecting to be hired again anytime soon. Blackballed is what it's called being excluded.

According to the Merriam-Webster Dictionary -The definition of blackball. (Entry 1 of 2) transitive verb. 1: to vote against especially: to exclude from membership by casting a negative vote. 2a: to exclude socially: ostracize.

This was definitely something that I would have to live down. It was during this time that I realized that family relationships is very important and vital to your survival. It's good to have some favors to call in. You also discover who has an ax to grind with you. Everybody communicates with you when you are not in need, but you lose a lot of friends and relatives when you are. I don't know if it's the fact that they don't know what to say to try to comfort you and not offend you, or if they stay away because you are so bitter as a result of what you are going through that you scare everyone away. People don't know how to approach you during really bad times. What are they going to say? How's the lawsuits going? Or maybe how's your sick husband doing? Or did you get another job yet? I had so many issues that I began to avoid people to save both of us the embarrassment. They didn't know what to inquire about and I didn't want to always have bad news to report. There are many important lessons to learn in the mist of controversy. One of them is that you have few friends. You will be able to identify your true friends when circumstances set you apart, the same will be true for your enemies. When you emerge from the battle you will have no doubt as to whom they are. There is nothing like being down in a foxhole with the enemy. Its your life or theirs. Suddenly you discover the value of yours, so you fight to keep it. Fox holes reveals cowards and heroes to the world, and they also introduces them to themselves. There is not a more ideal place that commands disrobing then in cramped quarters. Heat demands the shedding of outer garments. It forces us to reveal who we are right in the core of combat. A great warrior will become a more skillful fighter. On the other hand, a coward will, by the same pressures and forces, become more cowardly. James Allen quotes, "Circumstance does not make the man; it reveals him to himself." he could not have made a truer statement.

I found this to be exactly right.

Fellow employees who had experienced similar experiences with the company stuck their heads in the sand or straight up ran away. They were afraid that they were going to lose their jobs. I didn't wait around to track the people that I couldn't count on, but I understood. After all, these employees that had experienced Racial Bias were black, Hispanic and Indian male engineers. Where were they going to get equitable income from? They would also be blackballed, and they considered themselves lucky to have a job in the industry.

It was seven years and dozens of depositions later to settle with the company. They held out as long as they could in order to reduce the amount of the settlement demand. I felt a sense of accomplishment after the settlement was reached. I truly feel that because of what I had to endure, people of color was in a better position to follow suit if the company's Racial Bias policies were not instituted and enforced. I felt it was my responsibility to act, paving the way for stronger company policies that may be instituted that would weed out violators of Racial and Civil Rights laws within the company.

Chapter 15
Our Gain

2002 WAS A TOUGH YEAR AND ONE THAT ushered in change. The doctor was saying that it was going to take at least 18 months to see what kind of permanent brain and body damage Terry had sustained as result of the surgery. After 18 months Terry had a Comparison with Criterion Standards of Wechsler Adult Intelligence Scale-Revised (WAIS-R) test to measures the injury of severity coupled with other test which measured permanent Brain Damage. He scored a 62 IQ on the testing.

What does an IQ of 60 mean? An estimated 89 percent of all people with mental deficiencies have **I.Q.s** in the 51-70 range. An **I.Q.** in the 60 to 70 range is approximately the scholastic equivalent to the third grade. **IQ of 60** is significantly Mentally Handicapped, and in many cases be related to one who has Down Syndrome and or a Traumatic Brain Injury.

As stated by Human Rights Watch

We followed the doctor's orders as close as we could. Terry did everything he could to regain all his loses, to no avail. Paul said in

> ***2 Cor 12: 6-10 KJV***

> ***"For though I would desire to glory, I shall not be a fool; for I will say the truth: but now I forbear, lest any man should think of me above that which he seeth me to be, or that he heareth of me. And lest I should be exalted above measure through the abundance of the revelations, there was given to me a thorn in the flesh, the messenger of Satan to buffet me, lest I should be exalted above measure. For this thing I besought the Lord thrice, that it might depart from me. And he said***

unto me, My grace is sufficient for thee: for my strength is made perfect in weakness. Most gladly therefore will I rather glory in my infirmities, that the power of Christ may rest upon me. Therefore, I take pleasure in infirmities, in reproaches, in necessities, in persecutions, in distresses for Christ's sake: for when I am weak, then am I strong."

Terry actually had gone to the third heaven that Paul refers to in 2 Corinthians 12:1-5. He had to live with Frontal Lobe Brain Damage constant seizures, asphyxia, hypoxia, and that's just to name a few of the conditions that remained.

He truly understand what Paul was saying regarding revelations from the Lord and the enormous privilege of having traveled to heaven and spending time with Jesus, *"hearing unspeakable words, which it is not lawful for a man to utter,"* is definitely a reason to glory but balance and humility came in the suffering thereafter.

Terry worked so hard to come back. He had the spirit and courage of a Lion. He could almost taste recapturing his health. He would work so hard to regain ground, just to discover something new has jumped into the ring to challenge him. He held a good attitude about everything. God gave him a heavenly journey to give him the strength he needed for the days ahead. What a humble man he was. He was naturally a gentle man, but this made him even more so. Every time he fell down, he got back up. When the days got hard and the nights were long, he ran on ice. When your road is paved with ice and you know that it's a matter of time before you fall down, you run. Walking is not an option for you. You walk on ice when you know you can fall down and you are sure that you have the strength to pull yourself back up, before freezing. You run when there is no chance of you getting up if you fall down. Running helps you cover more ground, (distance) before you fall, with the hope that you have gained and maintained the speed necessary to propel you right into the ice-free area, thrusting you into the safety on the other side. We ran as fast as we could.

Chapter 16
The Things We Kept

Looking back over the years, I can truly say that we gained more than we lost. We learned lessons that we could not have possibly learned without those experiences. Priceless essentials for living this life with contentment like patience, brotherly love, and compassion. We learned peace, joy, hope, humility and unwavering faith thru suffering. We learned to humble ourselves before the workings and the will of God. We learned what is really important and worth fighting for in life. We learned that the most valuable things in life are not able to be brought, like unmerited love, understanding and compassion for others, a commitment to God, yourself and the people you love. We both learned that we could live without some things that we thought we could never live without. We learned that what God gives you, He wants you to have. And those gifts from God will be what each of us need, in order that we may grow thereby. Spiritual growth is the purpose of life. We grow towards His glory. Like the flower which grows reaching for the direction of the sun. We cannot grow without His light, and still blossom with His beauty. We learned that all growth is good. We learned how to rejoice in all things. We learned how to laugh. We learned that crying is not optional, and it was sometimes necessary. We discovered that we were in the process of learning how to live and die happy and continent. And it is good. We learned we could have Summer in the Winter, and Spring in the Fall. We found that without the spirit, the body is just a piece of flesh. Life is truly in the spirit. No, I would not trade my journey for anything. What we picked up along the way is invaluable. Warriors are critiqued through battles. Perseverance, endurance and the courage to win are ingredients necessary for a good old fashion fight. The things we learned through those experiences were well worth our losses. We gained far more than we lost.

One thing that we gained through this experience was a **greater love** and **respect** for each other. In marriage you really don't know the power of love and commitment that the couple has for each other, until you are tested in the areas of physical and psychological change. Change that could happen at any age will try the cohesiveness of the relationship. It happens when sexual intimacy is impossible, mental intelligence is impaired and physical prowess and agility is suddenly taken away from one partner. We leaned on Godly principles and our commitment to Him and His word to get through these trying times. It's easy to say, "I'm going to walk away because this is not what I signed up for". Terry was well mentally and physically when we got married. All it took for me to stay the course was putting myself in his shoes. How would I want him to treat me if I was in his condition? He rose in the morning and went to bed everyday calling my name. When he became brain damaged and he became mentally impaired, I became his mother and our relationship changed into just that. Overnight I had 3 children. Love is not to be thrown away but is all encompassing and becomes absolutely impartial to include the neediness of all parties, especially in times of necessity. Love turns into what you need it to be. Obligation exposes the intensity of love. *"Respect is not given, it is earned".* Quotes -Brian Dawkins

1 Corinthians 13:4-7 NKJV says,

"Love is patient, love is kind. It does not envy, it does not boast, it is not proud. It is not rude, it is not self-seeking, it is n love. **"Respect not given, it is earned". Quotes** *~Bot easily angered, it keeps no account of wrongs. Love takes no pleasure in evil but rejoices in the truth. It bears all things, believes all things, hopes all things, endures all things. Love never fails."*

This was written by Paul to Christians. He gives us a collection of fruit that is present as a result of love. Notice that he is not telling you that this fruit is the result of a specific type of love. He covers divine love regardless of what the relationship is.

What kind of love is Agape Love?

Agape is universal **love**, such as the **love** for strangers, nature, or God. Unlike storage, it does not depend on filiation or familiarity. Also called charity by Christian thinkers, **agape** can be said to encompass the modern concept of altruism, defined as **unselfish** concern for the welfare of others.

Romans 12:9-13 BSB says,

"Love must be sincere. Detest what is evil; cling to what is good. Be devoted to one another in brotherly love. Outdo yourselves in honoring one another. Do not let your zeal subside; keep your spiritual fervor, serving the Lord. Be joyful in hope, patient in affliction, persistent in prayer. Share with the saints who are in need. Practice hospitality."

God is clear with instructions to Christians on how we should treat other Christians and especially our own families. If you love them then you have done the whole law of Christ.

The second attribute we obtained as a result this experience, was patience. Patience is a virtue. It is a virtue because you need it in order to obtain certain things you are hoping to receive. Patience is the ability to tolerate delay in the face of suffering. We learned patience as a result of praying for physical healing. Having patience did not assure us that what we were praying for was going to happen, and it did not mean that whatever we did receive would happen the way we expected it to happen. Trouble produces patience within the Christian. Patience justifies the faith by which we have access of the grace by which we stand. It gives us confidence that the presence of God is with us. We were standing in a grace that is strong enough to uphold us. When patience is developed, we will have the ability to go through struggle and trouble practicing Godly moral values. When I say 'Godly moral values' I mean that we can go through hard-ship being honest, truthful and sincere. Having integrity, holding onto your moral and ethical principles. Being kind and considerate to others and treating them as such. While we were being tried, we were learning that the trying of our faith would develop patience in us.

James 1:2-4 KJV

My brethren count it all joy when ye fall into divers temptations; Knowing this, that the trying of your faith worketh patience. But let patience have her perfect work, that ye may be perfect and entire, wanting nothing.

Thirdly, we learned perseverance. We had to keep hoping and trying to beat what was fighting us. We knew this was something that we could not afford to allow to win by default, just because we gave up. We couldn't give in. We had too many people that we needed to care for, we had too many unfulfilled dreams to wake up. And what would we say about the ability of God. We chose to believe that God would do it any day now. We pushed through one day at a time. We took on one battle at a time hoping that we could win the war by little increments. We obtained courage in the mist of critical diagnosis, constant emotional turmoil and living in the fear of death knocking at the door daily. Many things could cause us to have to start all over. We had courage to pray and expect God to do for us what the doctors could not do. It took courage to fight our employers, The State of New York and the Hospital all at the same time. We had the courage to fight. As a matter of fact, we gained the courage because we had a family to save, a house to preserve and a legal precedence to set for the people who would suffer a fraction of what we had. In their future, we needed to give them something to reference. Without perseverance we would have had zero chance of winning this race. And absolutely nothing to testify about.

Everything slowed down. We put our lives on hold because life demanded it. We got behind God and God walked and talked us through every step. We became experts in waiting for everything and everybody. Patience is a virtue because it is something that you receive after you have suffered awhile.

After four years of Terry living at home, His health began to deteriorate requiring that he had 24-hour care. Terry had suffered an acute Myocardial Infraction. As a result, he underwent multiple stent procedures, eventually requiring quadruple bypass grafting. Following the surgery, he developed a post-operative sternal infection that required surgical debridement, during which, complications occurred. He then suffered with Frontotemporal Dementia, Hypoxic-ischemic encephalopathy, Tonic-clonic seizures, and spontaneous TIA – Transient Ischemic Attacks are called mini-strokes.

His fate was living with severe cognitive and physical disabilities which grew progressively worst.

The decision to choose a place for him was not an easy decision. After all, it was my decision to bring him directly home from the hospital and nurse him back to health. We both believed that God was going to give him a complete healing as a demonstration of how great God's healing power was for all the world to see. The sicker he got the more we believed that God was going to show himself strong on our behalf. Sometimes we have to trust God and his infinite wisdom when it comes to what is best for everybody involved. We wanted Terry well, but he once said to me, that if it had not been for what actually happened to him, he would still be worried all the time. He said that he had never had such peace in his life. And what happened to him was the best thing that could have ever occurred.

We learned to live separately, in two different residences but together. We learned that we could handle whatever life threw at us with God in the middle of us. We learned that we could not be separated because we were truly best friends and no matter what, we would be there for each other. We had each other's back. Why? Because we had made a covenant before God, and a responsibility to our little family to fulfill it. We were responsible for our own household's security and emotional well-being. Our only option was to stick together., being supportive of each other. And most of all to have patience with each other.

Ecclesiastes 4:9-12 NIV explains the advantage of having the support of your family to us...

9 Two are better than one, because they have a good return for their labor:10ForIf either of them falls down, one can help the other up. But pity anyone who falls and has no one to help them up 11 Also, if two lie down together, they will keep warm. But how can one keep warm alone? 12 Though one may be overpowered, two can defend themselves. A cord of three strands is not quickly broken.

You are better together. You have a better chance of surviving every situation that life can hand you.

The challenge was to be patient through our suffering. God tried us in so many ways, but he was faithful in every way.

The nursing facility was accommodating but it is important to keep the visits to your loved one almost daily, as often as possible for sure. Family members coming to visit will ensure higher quality care. Your relative will be better cared for by the staff if you are attentive. Also, it is a good idea to stagger the times of your visits. You really will not be able to get a good feel of what they are experiencing if you do not alternate your visits. Drop in anytime. You will gain all the insight you need if you give surprise visits.

After a long battle with illness Terry transitioned into heaven on January 2nd, 2015. After visiting heaven in 2001 he prayed fervently to return. Nothing was able to top what he experienced in heaven. No love came close to the love he experienced in the presence of Jesus Christ. I can try to convey what he told me to you but It's hard to put into words what I felt every time he spoke of the love of God. There was such a heavenly feeling that accompanied his experience, my description of it will always fall short of you actually being engulfed with such power yourself. God was always present and in the room for this testimony of Himself. He confirmed his own truth. I was overwhelmed with the love of God every time Terry told the story. He was sent back to substantiate and corroborate the existence of The Living God. A loving and caring God, a strong God who has the purpose and plan for your life in His very hand. No, your life is not unplanned, accidental, or without purpose. Everything you go through in life is for a reason. God wants all of us to be His.

2 Peter 3:8-9 KJV say,

"But, beloved, be not ignorant of this one thing, that one day is with the Lord as a thousand years, and a thousand years as one day. The Lord is not slack concerning his promise, as some men count slackness; but is longsuffering to us-ward, not willing that any should perish, but that all should come to repentance."

Gods' time is not our time. He will come when He is ready for us and believers should live in expectation of His return.

It would not be fair to reveal to you a tragedy that was so traumatic without telling you that God was faithful to balance our times of distress with blessings, so many blessings. He took care of us financially and allowed us to travel internationally extensively. God introduced us to His world. The beauty of the differences in the nations of the world that He created are phenomenal. By showing us these different cultures, we began to understand the sovereignty of God. His love for humanity and the diversity that He has established in the world. He revealed to us, that we are not all the same and our lives are different because he has willed it. He took our minds off our situation by putting our attention on His handiwork which was so beautiful and unique that we had to think on those things instead. We got a royal introduction to what God has done and what he was capable of doing without a doubt. Our minds and eyes were full of his glory. His glory took us through our low despondent valleys to the peaks, the summits of our mountains with excitement and exhilaration. We travel from the Great Wall in Beijing, China to the Vatican in Rome. From the streets of Barcelona, Spain, to Paris, France in the Spring of every year. Just to name a few countries we visited. God is a great God and He will be faithful in balancing the experiences of your life. These were demanding years, but they were filled with emotional riches. He doesn't give us more than we can bear. But he will always give us more than we expect. I'm a living witness!

Paul tells us in *Philippians 4:8 KJV* to change what you meditate on.

"Finally, brethren, whatsoever things are true, whatsoever things are honest, whatsoever things are just, whatsoever things are pure, whatsoever things are lovely, whatsoever things are of good report; if there be any virtue, and if there be any praise, think on these things."

In some of the most difficult days in my life God gave me another perspective.

In Conclusion

AFTER GOING THROUGH THESE ROUGH years in my life, I have come to the conclusion that I would not have the wisdom nor the knowledge that I have obtained, if I had not been exposed to it. I am grateful for it. The experience has allowed me to have the tools to minister to people who are desperate and despondent for lack of information. I have counseled many people who needed advice regarding Long Term Illness, Hospital Policies, Nursing Home admittance, Legal Guardianship, Medical Malpractice and... Racial Discrimination Litigation. I became a wealth of information on Healthcare guidelines, Alzheimer and Demetria care and our Insurance coverage policies. Elderly Care and resources became my expertise. Of course, Terry's story was much rougher than I express to you. For he and the family. There were many incidents that God helped me to forget as a protective shield to get me through them. Only to be referenced and remembered when necessary. I am sure of this one thing, Terry did not die before his time, and his faith stayed strong in the Lord. Yes, there were times that he got weak in his flesh. There were many times when he was afraid, very afraid. His mind was affected by his medical condition and his body was batter and racked with war scars and pain. But his love for people and God did not wavier. Terry loved everybody he met and everybody who met him, loved him. God confirmed his love for him by giving him the honor of spending 10 days with Him. Terry hung onto THAT experience for the rest of his life.

Life has a purpose for all of us. We are introduced and exposed to what we need in life to grow spiritually and help others to do the same. Terry ministered to countless dying people. You will not leave this life until you fulfill your purpose and fulfill God's purpose for your life.

What is your purpose?

Romans 8:28 KJV

"And we know that all things work together for the good to them that love God, to them who are the called according to his purpose".

REFERENCES

1. *https://www.hrw.org/reports/2001/ustat/ustat0301-01.htm*
2. *Matthew Henry's Commentary On The Whole Bible Complete and Unabridged in One Volume Copyright 1991 By Hendrickson Publishers, Inc. ISBN: 0-943575-32X*
3. *The Holy Bible King James Version Copyright 1976 By Thomas Nelson Nashville, Tennessee*
4. *Berean Study Bible – www.berean.bible*
5. *New International Version*
   Originally published: 1973
   Authors: Biblica, Ibs
      Revision: 1984, 2011
      Copyright: Copyright 1973, 1978, 1984, Biblica
6. *https://enduringword.com*

CPSIA information can be obtained
at www.ICGtesting.com
Printed in the USA
LVHW011030120121
675964LV00007BA/667